LIVING CULTURE

LIVING CULTURE

A values-driven approach to revitalising
your company culture

Jan Thornbury

with notes by Colin Sharman

RANDOM HOUSE

BUSINESS BOOKS

First published in 2000 by Random House Business Books,
Random House, 20 Vauxhall Bridge Road, London SW1V 2SA

Random House Australia (Pty) Limited
20 Alfred Street, Milsons Point
Sydney, New South Wales 2061, Australia

Random House New Zealand Limited
18 Poland Road, Glenfield
Auckland 10, New Zealand

Random House (Pty) Limited
Endulini, 5a Jubilee Road, Parktown 2193, South Africa

The Random House Group Limited Reg. No. 954009

Papers used by Random House are natural, recyclable products made from
wood grown in sustainable forests. The manufacturing processes conform to
the environmental regulations of the country of origin.

ISBN 0 7126 6959 0

Companies, institutions and other organizations wishing to make bulk
purchases of books published by Random House should contact their local
bookstore or Random House direct:
Special Sales Director
Random House, 20 Vauxhall Bridge Road, London SW1V 2SA

Tel 020 7840 8470 Fax 020 7828 6681

www.randomhouse.co.uk
businessbooks@randomhouse.co.uk

Typeset by SX Composing DTP, Rayleigh, Essex
Printed and bound in Great Britain by
Biddles Ltd, Guildford and King's Lynn

CONTENTS

RECOMMENDED READING

Collins, James C. and Porras, Jerry I., 'Building Your Company's Vision',
    Harvard Business Review, September-October 1996, Reprint 96501
Collins, James C. and Porras, Jerry I., *Built to Last: Successful Habits of
    Visionary Companies*, Random House Business Books, 2000
Deal, Terence and Kennedy, Allen, *Corporate Cultures: The Rites and Rituals
    of Corporate Life*, Penguin, 1988
Johnson, Gerry, 'Managing Strategic Change – Strategy, Culture and
    Action', *Long Range Planning*, Vol. 25, No. 1, 1992
Kotter, John P., *Leading Change*, Harvard Business School Press, 1996
Schein, Edgar H., *Organisational Culture and Leadership*, Jossey-Bass, 1993
Schein, Edgar H., *Organisational Psychology*, Prentice-Hall, 1988

PREFACE

by Stephen Butler, KPMG International Chairman
In my role I spend a lot of time talking with senior executives in many different businesses around the world. Interestingly, in recent years, there seems to be one main thing on everyone's mind – a common theme that underlies all their individual concerns and ambitions. The single most important issue for business leaders today is this: the speed of change. Why is change, and especially the unrelenting speed of change, so important?

The practical reason is that chief executive officers, managing directors and company presidents are now personally responsible for their business's shareholder value. Their jobs depend on it. If they don't steadily increase the value of their organisation for stakeholders, their leadership posts will simply be handed to someone else. And the only way to increase shareholder value is to introduce new ideas, or to re-invent existing ones, executing the changes quickly and flawlessly. Investors are not interested in what the organisation has achieved in the past, but only in what's new, exciting and different. With stakeholders focused on change, and CEOs focused on stakeholders, the whole organisation is driven by an insatiable thirst for 'the new': offshoot ventures, better solutions, new products and services, expanding markets – in a word, change. And with all the many changes going on in other businesses to divert stakeholders' attention, the faster the changes can be implemented, the better.

The second driver for high-speed business change is customer demand and competition. Customers are just as demanding as shareholders – and they have even less loyalty. Most customers these days are happy to go to any supplier, changing even from day to day in order to have the latest style or technology, the best price, or the most effective service. Indeed, most people are comfortable simultaneously using a range of different suppliers for even closely-related products or services, while still expecting complete dedication from each supplier in return, to ensure that they are a 'delighted' customer. To put it succinctly, it's a buyer's market, and there are always several new sellers coming onstream tomorrow to take away whatever buyers are around today. So businesses need to keep changing – in order to keep their existing customers interested, and continuously to attract new ones. They need to perceive the life cycle of each part of their business in terms of months rather than years or decades, and to maintain a hothouse atmosphere which is highly innovative and quick to market.

A third phenomenon driving the need for fast, effective change is the scarcity of skilled and experienced employees. To attract and keep the most able people, it is no longer enough to offer competitive remuneration, working conditions and benefits. The best people want to wake up each morning knowing that they're going to make a difference. This means putting them in charge of weird and wonderful new developments, radical 'out-of-the-box' thinking, or revolutionary developments that will transform the whole industry. Once again, change is king. Companies which resist change, which are wedded to traditional methods, which are not 'at the centre of things' – are tending to lose their most energetic, motivated people, and are having a hard time replacing them with equivalent talent. The same is true for staff at the top – the best executives are being headhunted away from the blue-chips into market-leading innovators and exciting new startups.

With today's shareholders, customers, and employees all preferring a creative, dynamic business environment to a steady, solid, conventional one, many companies are themselves seeking ways to be more like Silicon Valley start-ups than venerable bricks-and-mortar blue chips.

But what concerns all those business leaders around the world – the ones to whom I've been talking – is that although change appears exciting and attractive from the outside, inside the organisation it actually means a lot of painful upheaval, disruption, and displacement, and considerable insecurity for a great many individuals. While the stock exchanges, the markets, and the executive search firms are riding high on waves of continuous transformation – the vast majority of ordinary people who are pension and mortgage holders, mall shoppers, and nine-to-five employees still need sufficient stability and continuity in their working lives to pay their mortgages, raise their families, and plan their personal future with some certainty. How can the new ideal of month-by-month business change be reconciled with the mundane reality of decade-long home loans, families and careers? How can the organisation itself, which is made up of all those increasingly stressed individuals, survive the accelerating pace of business change?

The answer lies in this book. As it will explain, the best way to withstand speed and change on the surface is by creating something solid and permanent underneath. And for businesses, that something is a clear, strong company culture.

You will learn that there are three things you need to do to give vitality and strength to your organisation's culture: (1) Understand the existing culture, (2) Define a desired culture – including an inspiring mission and a set of supporting values, and (3) Align the business and individual behaviour with those values, so that the organisation starts to live the desired culture. The result will be an enduring, consistent and universal self-image for the organisation – a sense of purpose which everyone believes in and trusts, and which transcends constantly shifting share values, market life cycles, and senior executives.

Our long-term culture change programme at KPMG, even in just the few years it's been going since Colin Sharman launched it, is already having a positive stabilising effect – bringing the global organisation closer together, uniting its skills and knowledge, and making it more confident than ever about its future – all in a period when the firm is undergoing faster change than ever. Our stronger sense of purpose and unity is enabling us to compete extremely well against our massive 'Big Five' competitors in accountancy and consulting. It's also given us the confidence to be experimental and tailor our offerings with great speed and agility, in order to fend off the many niche practices springing up with narrowly-targeted services. The culture change has given us the sense of direction we needed to enter into creative alliances and ventures with other companies – for example, the advanced technology suppliers Cisco and Qwest – thereby creating enormous new business opportunities for KPMG. It's given our thousands of partners worldwide, the leaders of our firm, a much longer-term view of their role: a role that I call 'stewardship' of the business, whereby we turn over to the next generation a better firm than the one we inherited. And our new culture has given us the vision to become the leading innovators in our field, with cutting edge services, people and knowledge which our competitors can only strive to imitate.

In accordance with the ever faster pace of modern business, I am actually accelerating KPMG's culture change programme, so that we are now moving towards our goals even faster. I am encouraging everyone in the firm to transform themselves and the organisation as fast as they possibly can, to embrace our new mission and practice our values. I recognise that given the many different cultural and economic environments in which our firm operates across the world, specific practices will need to move at different speeds. But I also believe that certain key changes – like personal accountability, corporate-style governance, and infra-structure investment – can take place simultaneously everywhere.

The pace of change for KPMG, and indeed for everyone in the business world, is still rising, and I believe it will continue to do so for a long while yet. This makes it all the more important – both in business organisations everywhere and in our own personal ambitions – to find that calm in the centre of the storm, that culture of strong human values in the face of fleeting business fashions, that sense of permanence in the midst of relentless change.

TURNING THE TANKER

Introduction by Lord Sharman of Redlynch, KPMG International Chairman 1997–1999

For the first time in the history of commerce, multinational business organisations are able to promote themselves convincingly with one voice and purpose across the entire world. In large part, this is due to new telecommunications technologies such as the Internet, voicemail, and global mobile phones. These technologies are enabling businesses to appear and behave as though the world comprised a single, large business environment: one boundary-free, frictionless marketplace of suppliers, partners and customers, which has the potential to maximise the productivity and efficiency of economies everywhere. The economic benefits – as well as the social or environmental risks – of this perceived 'globalisation' of business and industry are widely acknowledged and much discussed. But what is less remarked upon is this: although globalisation has technological roots and economic drivers, the challenge of becoming a successful global business is primarily an issue not of technology or economics, but rather, of culture.

Why culture? With advances in technology, we find ourselves in a new, global, knowledge economy, where value resides overwhelmingly in intellectual property, human wisdom and intangible goods. Any organisation which does not effectively grow, manage and maintain its corporate knowledge in this global economy will fall behind. So of course it is important that we have systems to catalogue our knowledge, share it, sort it and make it instantly available at the desk top. However, far too frequently, organisations concentrate only on installing the finest technology systems and never seem to realise their full benefit. Why? Because even though they might have the best knowledge management system in the world, they cannot persuade the people who are using it to share what is locked up in their grey matter. The critical success factor in determining how effectively an organisation manages its corporate knowledge is not a technology issue. It is a cultural issue – all to do with creating, encouraging and sustaining the right attitudes and patterns of human behaviour. In short, knowledge management is more about psychology than technology. It is much more about the values and behaviours at large in the business than about IT and communication systems, important as these may be.

An understanding of economics is also not enough to help businesses survive globalisation. The reality is that the commercial world is not really one cohesive business environment. As you travel from one country to another, you are likely to confront very different or even antagonistic economic behaviours, values and traditions – each influenced by the local society, history and customs. Between any two countries, there will be differences in, for example: how business is conducted, the way staff are treated, ease of access to skills and technology, logistical issues such as transport and infrastructure, how business is financed, how alliances are built, and what local regulatory controls are in place. Moreover, each bilateral relationship between two economies is uniquely moulded by the historical and political relationship between their peoples. Doing business across several different countries, let alone the whole world, can be a bewildering experience.

Although the business environment can differ dramatically from place to place, it is true that customers everywhere are becoming more alike in what they expect from the products and services they buy. Nearly everyone, from Alaska to Zimbabwe, will tell you that they expect to receive for their money: 100% quality, the latest available technology and functionality, highly competitive pricing, 24-hour-a-day access to information, and a tailored, personal standard of service. But because the way business is conducted varies so greatly, whether or not these universal expectations can be met in a particular location is far from certain.

Regardless of how 'global' an international business may appear, the experience of its customers depends to a great extent on where the customer happens to live or work.

To counteract the effects of geographic differences, to rationalise business practices and policies, and to satisfy universal customer expectations, businesses have only one practical weapon: the strength, effectiveness and integration of their corporate culture.

When I began my tenure as International Chairman of KPMG in February of 1997, it was clear that we needed to take stock of where we were in creating a global business. KPMG was a well-established brand among the then 'Big Six' accounting and consultancy firms. We were certainly international, with a presence in 157 countries and around 92,000 staff from all parts of the world, but were we global? It was a full ten years since the merger of KMG and Peat Marwick International set up a worldwide federation of their jointly held 800 member firms under the one new brand, KPMG. Although the merged organisation was a federation in theory, in practice its operations were not really all that different from the other five big professional services firms. What was different from the other firms was the way KPMG was run: its management structure was indeed a federation – there was little central control and decision-making was primarily carried out by boards and committees comprising representatives of the larger national practices. We looked more like a loose federation than a unified, global firm.

In 1997, due to various factors, including consolidation in the marketplace for accountancy and consulting, KPMG was generally perceived by the media and many clients as being somewhat behind its major competitors in its efforts to globalise. I likened the international firm to an oil tanker, chugging along too slowly in the ocean of globalisation. It was big, cumbersome and slow to move. Moreover, given the federal nature of its governance, it didn't have much of a rudder to steer by. We needed to turn the tanker, to take the quickest and most effective route to globalisation, but we did not have the power at the centre to direct it on this path. I concluded that there must be more subtle and more effective ways to change KPMG than grasping power at the centre – a process which would have involved extensive restructuring. Anyhow, I knew that it wasn't the right time to be tinkering with the firm's structure. The negotiations needed to restructure a firm with over 6,000 partners would have taken up too much of our attention and energies, at a time when we needed to devote ourselves primarily to enhancing our standing in the marketplace. So the question was: How can you turn a tanker without altering the rudder? What could we do, short of changing the structure of the firm, to transform 800 fairly autonomous KPMG practices into a global business able to build relationships and operate seamlessly across boundaries?

To find an answer, I first thought about other large businesses which at least appeared to operate successfully as worldwide organisations. The first one that came to mind was the fast-food company, McDonald's – surely one of the best-known global brands in any industry. Despite being a huge international franchise business, with thousands of autonomous operators in over 100 countries, to the outside world the company appears to be more or less the same everywhere. The customer always knows exactly what to expect: the same look, the same level of service, the same menu (perhaps with some local additions), the same processes for sales, and the same quality of product, guaranteed by McDonald's shared supply system and infrastructure. Very few customers, if they did not know otherwise, would guess that McDonald's is a franchise operation.

I felt that if McDonald's could create something which looked like a truly global organisation, even if it was not structured in that way, then so could KPMG. In general business terms, what McDonald's had, that we didn't, were five things: a strong, consistent brand; common products and services; uniform business processes; a shared infrastructure and, perhaps most importantly, a single, strong corporate culture. I felt that if we could create these five things for KPMG, our unique skills and experience would shine through, and our increased ability to operate globally would enable us to surge ahead of all our major competitors.

The global integration of KPMG was especially urgent for our newer service sectors like consulting, whose multinational clients wanted us to draw all our diverse local expertise into one holistic view. Our consulting advice to multinational clients could have value only if it built on a truly global perspective – a consistent understanding of broad regional and international economic trends, cross-border trade, and worldwide business networks.

But at the same time I was aware that an integrated global firm would need to remain sensitive and responsive to each and every local community where we operate. One of KPMG's great strengths, which enables its member practices to retain many loyal clients and to win thousands of new engagements, is their comprehensive knowledge and experience of all the world's local business environments: for example, local tax and accounting practices, local business customs, laws and regulations, and the local market and infrastructure.

Globalisation was top of the agenda when I was appointed as the firm's International Chairman. In the first weeks of my tenure, I needed to consider how our global ambitions might be implemented without throwing KPMG's complex federal structure into a distracting turmoil. Without making structural changes to the federation, somehow all our people needed to *feel* part of a global firm, to our clients we needed to *look* like a global firm, in delivering our professional services we needed to *act* like a global firm, and we needed to organise our collective know-how so that we could *think* like a global firm. I concluded that our aim should be to create what I called a *virtual* global firm – one which displayed all the key characteristics of a global company, but without needing a wholly centralised management structure, and without losing the distinctive benefits of local knowledge and experience. In brief, we had to focus not on structural changes, but on the changes to our culture and our operations which would enable us to provide consistent and high quality service to our clients, all around the world.

I developed these ideas into a proposition which became known as the 'Virtual Firm' strategy, the key tenets of which said, that instead of making structural changes, KPMG would focus its immediate globalisation efforts on:

- being clear about what we stood for: a shared set of *values* worldwide
- defining what we did (and didn't do): consistent *core services*
- agreeing how we did it: common *business processes*
- creating a robust, centrally managed, global *infrastructure* to support all of the above

Because culture permeates everything, and is a key factor in the success of any major project, I felt that the values work was the most critical and urgent of these four tasks. I also knew that although a small number of KPMG's national practices had already begun to work on values-related issues – Steve Butler in particular had been an exemplary leader of cultural and behavioural change in the US practice – in general there would be less 'demand' for it in the day-to-day activities of the firm. I knew that culture change for KPMG globally would not take place at all unless I made it a priority, a process driven by the firm's leaders internationally.

In May 1997, I presented the 'Virtual Firm' strategy to KPMG's International Council (the firm's ultimate governing body) at the first of its meetings which I was to chair in my new role. As the Council discussed these ideas, the consensus was that such initiatives were long overdue. Everyone agreed that a unified culture, globally consistent core services, common business processes, and a shared infrastructure across our many international practices was absolutely vital to enhance the competitiveness of the firm – even if it was going to be a challenge to achieve such things.

With the help of my team, the Council immediately set to work on our values and on our core services, but the more we talked about what this new 'virtual global firm' should be like, the more confused we became. It was evident before long that we had no single, clear idea about the firm's core purpose – its true identity – and our deeper aspirations. Our existing mission statement – which was mainly about being the world's leading accounting and consulting firm, with an emphasis on service definitions, quality and professionalism – lacked any forward vision or historic depth. All we knew was that we wanted to be as effective as McDonald's in globalising the business – although we obviously didn't want to become the McDonald's, per se, of professional service companies. McDonald's had a vision and values well suited to its market and ambitions. We needed our own vision and values – suited to our particular market and stating very clearly what KPMG is all about. More work needed to be done on our mission as well as our values.

We therefore took a long, hard look at who and what we really were. What we discovered was that KPMG essentially comprises a set of assets – namely our clients, people, and knowledge – and that our activities are centred around these assets. In searching for a phrase which encapsulated KPMG's reason for being, someone put forth the notion that the firm exists simply to 'exploit its assets', but this seemed to me too mechanistic in tone, lacking humanity – unacceptable for a business so dependent upon its people. Eventually we came round to a form of words that seemed to describe our purpose perfectly, which acknowledged our assets and maintained a human emphasis: we agreed that KPMG exists '*to turn knowledge into value for the benefit of its clients, people and communities*'. This simple statement of purpose seemed to contain all the questions and answers about who we were: What does KPMG comprise? Clients, people, and knowledge. What does KPMG do? It creates value. How does it do that? It turns knowledge into value. Who benefits? Its clients, its own people and the communities within which it operates. In addition to altering the wording of our mission, we encapsulated our new statement of purpose in a brief, memorable phrase which would guide us throughout the firm. We did this by restricting the message to 'how' KPMG works: 'Turning knowledge into value'. We felt this was straightforward enough to be understood and acted upon by every single person in the firm, irrespective of their role, or where they were in the world.

There was of course still much more to do. In particular, we needed to develop and implement the values which would complement our new statement of purpose and help in driving our strategic agenda. Over a period of about a year, through extensive international consultation, and involving as many KPMG people as possible, we researched our existing culture and, using our new mission and the notion of our three assets to guide us, defined what needed to change. The work concluded with another clear statement, derived from our new mission. This statement said that, above all else, KPMG believes in adding value to the firm's assets: clients, people and knowledge. To add value to our clients, the statement explained: *We are passionate about working with our clients to deliver exceptional value.* In other words, we will offer our clients an outstanding, value-adding service, and we will build with them robust, lasting relationships. As concerns our second asset, we want to see '*our people flourish and realise their full potential*'. We want each person to see KPMG as the place where their highest aspirations can be realised. At KPMG, work is rewarding, career development is actively managed and teamwork is paramount to personal success. We also state that '*We continuously extend the frontiers of our shared knowledge*'. Knowledge is our collective experience, skills, tools and information. It is precious to us, and we all have an obligation to contribute to our knowledge base as well as benefiting from our shared learning.

Of course we knew that our new statement of values, no matter how widely shared, would not make a difference to KPMG if we did not put anything in place to implement it. The final phase of KPMG's culture change programme – which is still ongoing – is the roll-out of a comprehensive 'Values Implementation Toolkit' across KPMG's practices worldwide. This gives practical advice and assistance to our people around the world in designing and running local culture change programmes. In this way, it helps people in our 157 local firms to understand, promote and 'live' our values. The implementation effort has now moved away from the centre and is in the hands of the senior partners from our practices around the world. I have been impressed by how they are putting the toolkit to use. I have seen some of my closest colleagues embrace values-based leadership wholeheartedly and become passionate drivers for culture change. Mike Rake, the Chairman of KPMG's UK firm, is just one such example. I will never forget the UK firm's annual conference in 1998, when under his leadership, fifteen hundred KPMG partners and senior managers worked for two whole days to agree how they would change KPMG's culture – starting with their own behaviour. Other examples are too numerous to mention, suffice to say that for many of our practices around the world, culture is top of the agenda, and on my visits I have seen how the values are worked on, discussed and brought to life at a local level.

Looking back on the whole global culture initiative – whose aim, again, was to help make KPMG succeed as a global enterprise – I can say with certainty that it has already had a significant impact on the firm and its performance. KPMG is no longer playing catch-up with its main competitors; indeed, the firm is leading the field in many key areas. Because we are increasingly perceived as a truly global enterprise – moreover, one with in-depth local expertise – we are winning more engagements from large multinational clients than ever before. People in the firm are more excited and enthusiastic about the future than they have been for years. And our new knowledge management system is the envy of the professional services industry, and a model for other industries besides.

But the firm is not resting on its laurels. The creation of KPMG's new global culture is an ongoing process – driven by Steve Butler, the new International Chairman, with the same vigour and focus. As long-term projects, all culture change programmes require firm, forcible and constant leadership. Steve provides that leadership. Indeed, he already has a successful record of achieving lasting and significant culture change in KPMG's US practice. He has shown that he is prepared to get tough when needed, and to reward those who truly embody the new culture. His commitment, drive and powerful sponsorship are exactly what the global firm now needs.

With the benefit of hindsight, there are of course things I might have done differently during my tenure to speed up KPMG's globalisation process. I was so concerned not to tie up the firm's energies in negotiating a new management structure, that I avoided making even the few structural changes which – while causing very little disruption – might have further accelerated the implementation of the firm's globalisation strategy. Specifically, I could have moved more swiftly to form an International Executive Team to lead these efforts. Similarly, I clung to the idea of the 'Virtual Firm' perhaps too long. What we needed was not only a 'virtual' organisation that exhibited the desired characteristics and behaviours on its surface, but a real organisation which lived out, day-to-day, and in every location, the core values beneath these desired behaviours. The organisation needed to reflect in its real-life structures, decisions and processes the global vision and culture which we were creating. I realise now that in the end, the two go hand-in-hand: you need to create the organisation to support your culture as well as creating the culture to revitalise your organisation.

In the following pages, Jan Thornbury – who led KPMG's work on values, and with her innovative tools and techniques, set in motion the culture change programme across the global firm – explains why values and culture are the keys to improving any kind of organisation. She describes in depth many of the approaches we used in KPMG and this provides valuable insights for anyone undertaking culture change. (Her text is interrupted by my occasional comments, mainly to help to illustrate her points with instances from our own culture change experience.) Jan explains how to understand an existing corporate culture, the practical steps you can take to change that culture, and most importantly, how to get an organisation to 'live' its new values. There are few organisations, of any size or kind, which cannot benefit from this important new knowledge.

Chapter 1

THE IMPORTANCE OF CULTURE

The man reached into his top pocket and drew out a glossy little card.

'And these are our values,' he said, handing me the card.

I turned the card over in my hand. The words of his company's values statement were certainly inspiring. But if everyone from his organisation really did live and breathe those values, why did he have to hand them to me on a piece of paper? Surely I would have seen them already in his behaviour. And anyway, as his potential customer, I didn't need to see a written-down commitment to outstanding service. I just needed to see outstanding service.

Culture is in fashion in management circles. Almost every senior-level job description has something about 'culture change' tacked on to the end. This is just one of many books on corporate culture which you might have browsed through in the bookshop. So why is it, that when culture is so widely discussed and written about, it is still so poorly understood? Why do organisations invest so much in trying to change their cultures when the fruit of their efforts is often a finely crafted values statement which just makes you want to yawn?

The trick which is so often missed is to translate the glossy values statement into the real life of the organisation: to ensure that the new values become part of the living culture, and to ensure that people are living according to that culture.

There are substantial benefits to be gained through strengthening and revitalising your organisation's culture. All you need to do is bridge the gap between theorising about culture change and actually making it real. This book bridges that gap. We start off here with the theory and then go on to explain how it can be translated into practice, using the real-life story of KPMG and how it fared on the path to true culture change.

Keep your cards close to your chest

Culture is obviously not about little cards in the top pockets of your sales force. But what *is* it all about? Before we launch into detailed hypotheses, let us first consider, at a very high level, what organisational culture is.

All organisations and groups have a culture. As an outsider, you will form an impression of an organisation's culture as soon as you walk in. This will largely be based on what you see and hear. For example, suppose you had an appointment at a big law firm in New York – you would most likely enter a highly polished foyer, be led to a beautifully furnished meeting room, drink good coffee from porcelain cups, consult with smartly dressed, articulate people and, a few weeks later, receive an invoice for a large amount of money printed on creamy letterhead. What would your impressions be? From what you had seen and experienced, you would perhaps have formed a view that the law firm is professional, conservative, successful, high quality and expensive.

You would not expect to encounter an environment similar to the law firm if, for example, you visited a small design company in Paris, or a newspaper's offices in London. They are engaged in a completely different line of work and there are obvious reasons why each will have its own, unique atmosphere, look and attitudes.

It is easy to see why organisations which are engaged in different activities look and feel different. The surprise comes when you find that organisations which you would expect to be *similar* also have a completely different 'feel'. For example, both IBM and Hewlett Packard are highly successful, global companies. Both are in the IT business and both recruit from the same pool of talent. Based on this, you would expect them to be very alike, but there are few IT managers who would have trouble telling them apart. Any customer or employee of either organisation will tell you, not that one is good and the other bad, but that they just 'feel' different. Think of airlines – suppose you take two flights: one with Lufthansa and the other with Virgin. Both are reputable airlines. Both will get you safely and comfortably to your destination. But each has a distinctive 'style' and you will inevitably prefer one over the other, depending on your particular taste. Even organisations which to you look and feel similar might be perceived differently by others. For example, when I crave a hamburger I don't particularly care whether I go to McDonald's or Burger King. However, my five-year-old nephew could write a thesis (if he could write at all, that is) on the merits of one over the other. So why do organisations which you would expect to be similar often *feel* so different? It all comes down to culture.

By culture we mean the values, assumptions, behavioural patterns and observable attributes which we associate with a particular organisation or group. Every group, irrespective of its size or type, will have its own, unique culture. An obvious example is *national* culture. Societies have well-established organising principles, beliefs, customs and characteristics which have developed over time. These are often exaggerated in the stereotypical views we have of particular nations: fiery Italians, reserved English, polite Japanese and so on. Stereotyping does not apply to every *individual* person: most of us could find among our acquaintances examples of serene Italians, gregarious English people and rude Japanese (hang on, I've *never* met a rude Japanese person). But stereotypes do seem to hold true with more general national characteristics. Step into a few countries as a foreigner and you will soon feel those differences. There are definite behaviour patterns and beliefs which are unique to each national culture. Customs are also part of national culture. Sometimes national customs are so deeply ingrained that they persist even when people no longer agree with them. For example, the caste system in India lingers on today even though many people outside and inside the country believe it to be outdated. It has been a part of the country's cultural heritage for centuries and could not be abolished overnight, even if the will to do so was there. Culture is enduring and goes very deep.

In the past, culture has been the domain of anthropologists, who related it to national or tribal characteristics. Today we apply many of the same concepts to organisations. Just as nations have their own unique cultures, all organisations have a 'system' of values, philosophies and accepted rules about 'the way we do things around here'. In any business, employees generally conform to these accepted standards and, whether consciously or not, subscribe to the company's values.

Culture is a feature of organisations outside the business world too: for example, any club has an established culture and if you want to be accepted you need to make sure you adhere to the (often unwritten) rules. For example, try turning up in a scruffy pair of jeans at an English country golf club if you want to feel out of place. It's probably more important to look respectable than it is to be able to play golf. Even your own family will have a unique culture: a shared set of beliefs and a fairly rigid pattern of behaviours (against which you probably rebelled as a teenager).

As an individual, you will be a member of many different groups – your nation, your family, your place of work, your social circles and so on. Each of these groups will have its own, unique culture and you will be expected to 'fit in'. If you want to be accepted, you will need to adapt your behaviour to conform with the culture. This does not necessarily mean you will have to transform your entire personality – it is often easy to conform, especially if you buy into the values and behaviours of the group. Even if you don't wholeheartedly subscribe to the group's culture, it is often no great effort to conform with lesser rules or for limited periods of time. For example, you might be an old rocker at heart, but the chances are, you could still manage to squeeze into a business suit and tie if you landed a job at an investment bank. In some situations however, you may find that you cannot adapt sufficiently to cultural pressures. Most of us have at some time taken on a job with a company or joined a club where it was just too difficult to fit in. If you find that you can't adapt to the culture of a particular group, you will have only two choices: you can stick it out and continue to feel uncomfortable or, more likely, you can leave and go and find another group where you feel more at home.

Culture or cult?

Sometimes I have encountered people who say that the company for which they work has no culture. Having just stated categorically that all organisations have a culture, let's explain what they mean.

People who claim their organisation has no culture are actually expressing a frustration with a culture which is termed *weak*. Corporate cultures can be 'strong' or 'weak':

- A *strong* culture is one in which people share and deeply believe in the values of the organisation. Because of this, they gladly conform with patterns of behaviour which are in keeping with those values.
- In a *weak* culture, the organisation's values may not be clearly articulated. Even if they are, the employees may not genuinely buy into them, or they may feel a conflict between their personal values and the interests of the organisation. Consequently, there is no sense of shared beliefs and people can get away with behaving in a way which contradicts the values.

In a weak culture, people are often frustrated by inconsistencies and lack of direction. A strong culture, on the other hand, can sometimes be cult-like. People who enter an organisation with a strong culture who do not buy into the company's values often feel uncomfortable and ostracised.

An example of an organisation with a strong culture is the Walt Disney Corporation. I have a friend who worked there for a while. Most of his colleagues were infected with the Disney 'magic' and pursued happy and successful careers with the organisation. My friend could not get into it though, and left shortly after joining. He could not suspend his natural cynicism (well, he *is* English . . .) to imbibe Disney's cult-like optimism. He felt out of place and was relieved to go. He is someone who is talented and passionate about his work, and has since made a great career elsewhere. Should Disney be sorry to lose him? No. Disney is an organisation where it is of paramount importance to keep the dream alive, and that requires full buy-in to its values. However talented an individual might be, if they don't fit in, it is not worth compromising a strong culture to retain them.

> I like to think of corporate culture as 'The way we do things round here'. The way things are done in an organisation can be either clear and obvious, or vague and subtle, but the power of culture should not be underestimated. When Peat Marwick International merged with Klynveld McClintock Gesellschaft to form KPMG in 1987, both had strong cultures and there were, inevitably, tensions between the two. We did not recognise then how important it was to resolve any issues of culture clash, and I believe that the fragmentation which still dogged KPMG International in 1997 had its roots in our failure to fully address these issues. Mergers can fail when the differences between two strong cultures are not reconciled. The KPMG merger succeeded, but there is no doubt that we could have handled it a lot more effectively.

Where does culture come from?

How do particular corporate cultures arise? Understanding how cultures originate and grow is key to seeing how they can be changed.

In a few cases, the culture is wilfully created by the founders of the organisation. A well-known example of this is the technology giant, Hewlett Packard, which was founded in 1938 by Bill Hewlett and Dave Packard. Right at the company's inception, when these two were running the operation from a garage in California, they developed an inspirational statement of purpose and values known as the 'HP Way'. It was intended as a set of guiding principles for the organisation and reflected very much their personal beliefs. Hewlett and Packard had a clear sense of purpose for their company: to make a technical contribution to the world. They also shared a strong set of values which were to do with respecting the individual, having a responsibility to the community and providing affordable quality for their customers. As time progressed, the founders and leaders of Hewlett Packard reinforced this culture through their decisions and actions, so that it became second nature to the generations of employees that followed. Today, over fifty years later, the HP Way has barely changed and is still passionately adhered to in a company which has now grown beyond recognition and extended across the globe.

However, few organisations could claim that their founders gave the corporate culture a second thought during the early years. In the majority of companies, the culture evolves in a less planned manner. In most cases, it is 'learned' over time in the following way: The culture originates with a set of unconscious beliefs held by the founders and leaders of the organisation. These beliefs are applied to day-to-day situations. If the application of a particular belief repeatedly leads to success, then that belief will come to be regarded as 'right' for the organisation. With continued reinforcement in this way, it will become embedded in the organisation's culture. The converse is also true. If the practice of a particular belief consistently leads to failure, then it will, in time, be dropped from the system. Thus the unique system of values and behaviours which comprises a particular culture is usually a consequence of how initial beliefs have been modified by experience.

Let's illustrate this with a simplified example: Suppose in a sales organisation, people started off believing that they should be scrupulously honest with their customers. However, suppose that time after time when they were entirely honest with their customers, they lost the sale, while when they were not completely open they were more successful. After a while, they would come to realise that being scrupulously honest might not be the best way to win customers. Sooner or later, they would unconsciously drop the belief about being honest from the system and replace it by some other, not necessarily dishonest, but certainly different belief about how to win customers.

In more mature organisations, culture is like a long-established habit. People might not know its origins, but they tend to behave pretty much in keeping with its standards. We can draw a parallel with the beliefs that you apply unconsciously in your own daily life. You too, as a child, will have learned values and behaviours which are particular to your family or your surroundings, and which you will practise without question as long as the environment does not require you to change. If the environment does require you to change, it will take time for you to learn to apply new values. Not only that, but you will not be starting with a blank slate: you will also have to get out of the habit of applying your old values. This is difficult to do and often means that you will have to learn the hard way – by seeing that your old values repeatedly lead to failure or missed opportunities.

Just as with individuals, organisations need to 'learn' their new culture. This requires breaking old habits, and repeatedly receiving positive confirmation that the new way of doing things really does lead to better outcomes.

Values are for inside
The mistake which the man with his values in his jacket pocket made was to give me, a customer, a copy of his company values statement. Values are something for inside the organisation. They are there to guide employees. Customers do not need to see the company values statement. They see the brand and image which the organisation presents to the outside world, they see the quality of products and services, and they see how people in the organisation interact with them. On this basis they will make up their minds. Of course there are extremes. No one would hire 'Axe-Murderers R Us' to do their babysitting. But apart from this, the truth is that customers don't really care about the values statements of their providers. They do not pore over corporate values statements and say:

'Oh dear, Company X wants to consistently exceed my expectations but Company Y wants to continually surprise and delight me – which is it to be, which is it to be?'

Customers might not care about what the values of a particular organisation *state*, but they do, of course, care about whether they see those values *in action*. So if Company X truly delivers on its values, while Company Y does not, customers will automatically choose the former. Likewise, many people boycott organisations whose actions undermine commonly accepted values, for example by exploiting human or animal rights or disruption of the environment.

Values statements are only relevant to people inside the organisation. Of course, since people inside are also exposed to the image and brand presented outside the organisation, internal values and external image should be congruent. In other words, there is no point claiming to the outside world that your business is innovative, dynamic and wacky if its values on the inside are really all about being solid and safe and sticking to the rules. In cases like this, employees justifiably become cynical, regarding the company's image as meaningless hype.

Not just a fad: Good reasons for changing your culture
Corporate culture has been the darling of management gurus for about the past decade, with many businesses investing in culture change programmes in the hope that it will make them more competitive, efficient and successful. Tom Peters once said:

'I do a fair amount of corporate culture consulting. It's one of the more acceptable forms of stealing in the 1990s.'

Indeed, culture change has acquired a reputation as something of a management fad and a perfect excuse for management consultants to rip off their clients. However, this is more of an indictment on the *way* culture change efforts have been carried out than on the benefits which true change can bring.

So why is culture so important?

First of all, the business world is changing radically. At the beginning of the 21st century, we face an environment in which technology enables us to think, work and act in ways which we never could have imagined five or ten years ago. As boundaries fall away, organisations are becoming more fluid, with structures and processes that shift continually in response to customer demand. Companies need to be flexible in their use of resources, to be able to succeed in the virtual world and to operate seamlessly across the globe. Traditional structures and management methods will no longer suffice when it comes to maintaining cohesion in such increasingly flexible organisations. Instead, they will depend on a clear sense of purpose and values to keep their sense of identity and unity. In other words, culture will be the glue that holds together the modern organisation.

People are also developing different attitudes to work. Already, most people expect to have multiple careers and don't feel they need to be 'looked after' by an organisation. The coming generation of employees will have difficulty *imagining* the concept of company loyalty, never mind displaying it. Talented people know they are in great demand and will need something more than salaries and perks to keep them happy. Organisations will need to offer them inspiration, something to believe in and a sense of purpose. Already people are making decisions to join organisations – or not – on the basis of the company culture. Other considerations such as salary, benefits and stock options are all too easy to match.

Clearly, as we look at trends, we see that culture change will not be a fad to be ignored until it goes away. In fact it will become even *more* important to the organisations of the future. But what about today?

In the present business world, culture change is often carried out on the flimsiest of grounds. It is regarded as a 'good thing to do', but people struggle to pinpoint the benefits it might bring. In fact, culture change is one of the most powerful means of improving an organisation's performance in every sense. A considerable amount of research exists to support this view, one of the more conclusive studies being the work of Collins and Porras (1994), which shows that organisations with strong cultures do better than their peers in all respects – not only do they exhibit vastly superior financial performance, they also have a better record of endurance, innovation and reputation.

There are distinct, tangible benefits to be gained through improving and strengthening a corporate culture. It is not difficult to see why an organisation with a strong set of shared values would do better than one with a weak culture. In a strong culture, people all understand and believe in what the company stands for, and are clear about how that translates into their day-to-day behaviour. The result will be a highly motivated workforce, engaged in pursuing the same goals. The clarity gained from a shared sense of purpose and values liberates people to act on their own initiative. A strong culture is the key to achieving that elusive thing which business leaders today yearn to instil in their staff: empowerment.

In a strong culture, there is not much dependence on any particular leader because people *already* believe in the organisation and align themselves to it. The leader therefore does not have to work a miracle to provide direction and motivation. Companies with strong cultures tend to be resilient to changes in leadership. In a weak culture, people are less clear about what they need to do and how to do it, so they tend to be much more dependent on leaders. They need a tighter hand on the reins. Otherwise they may be inclined to pursue their personal agendas rather than aligning themselves with the goals of the organisation, or may waste time and energy trying to work out the 'right' way to do things. We all know that leaders don't last forever, so it seems that unless you want your organisation to fall to bits when your great leader retires, a strong culture is the preferred option.

'Change' has become a management buzz-word and I confess to being thoroughly sick of hearing it. But we do live in a turbulent world, and that requires us to be able to change swiftly and surely. Too swiftly perhaps – most companies don't even finish one major change programme before the next starts, and the next, and the next. Change programmes seem to be built on the shifting sands of the last change programme – no wonder we're all confused. Anyone who has studied even the rudiments of mathematics knows that you can't solve an equation if all the factors are variable. You need a constant if you want to find a solution. An organisation's core values provide the constant in the change equation. They provide certainty around which everything else – strategies, structures, people, processes and systems can change. Someone once described core values to me as 'the pin that holds the pendulum'. In other words, they are the focal point around which everything else can range freely. Core values provide focus, direction and essential and enduring guidance. Organisations with a powerful set of core values do not have to spend time wondering what is permanent and what can be changed. Their decisions are informed by their values. In this way, a strong culture helps organisations change more surely and swiftly.

An organisation's culture can definitely change – it's not a question of whether it can change, but how best to go about it. I've always been inspired by the massive culture change undertaken by British Airways under Colin Marshall. BA transformed itself in only a few years from a lumbering state-owned bureaucracy into a dynamic, customer-driven enterprise. If such a radical conversion could be managed so successfully there, then there is surely hope for the rest of us.

Globalisation and growth are among the key challenges facing organisations today. For companies which are expanding geographically, it is a challenge to align the beliefs and behaviours of people from different nationalities across the world. And, as if this wasn't difficult enough, while the *global* organisational culture might need strengthening, at the same time sensitivity to the *local* culture needs to be maintained. 'Think global, act local' might be a well-worn management cliché, but it is valid nonetheless. Globalisation is just one contributing factor to an even bigger cause of management headaches around the world: the issue of managing diversity. Globalisation means that business leaders are trying to bring together people from different *national* cultures. Meanwhile, many find that they are also trying to bring together different *organisational* cultures, as a result of mergers and acquisitions. Most of us have heard horror stories about 'culture clashes' when companies merge and the failure statistics are dire. And there is yet more complexity: in addition to national and organisational cultural diversity, many organisations are diverse in their own right, employing people from multiple professional cultures and skill areas. How do you really get your IT people to be business focused? How do you really get doctors to respect the decisions of hospital managers? And so on. The ability to manage diversity is becoming more and more important. Leaders have to become increasingly skilled at juggling multiple cultures: geographic, organisational and professional. An understanding of what can and should be aligned in the culture, and what should remain diverse, is essential. A 'must-have' quality of leaders in business today is sensitivity to cultural issues.

The present day business world provides us with plenty of reasons why culture is important. But what about the legacy of the past? Many organisations are seeking to improve their corporate cultures in the aftermath of the 1980s and 90s waves of downsizing, performance improvement (which is usually just another word for downsizing) and total quality management. They hope that culture change will enable them to motivate and retain their remaining, change-bludgeoned staff. They want to show their staff that, in spite of all that has happened, they are still the company's most highly valued asset. They hope that through culture change, staff will become energised, happy and inspired. To achieve this end, culture change, though difficult enough, is probably still cheaper than therapy.

In summary, whether an organisation is preparing itself for the future, trying to succeed in the present, making up for its past or maybe even doing all three, there are plenty of reasons for trying to revitalise, strengthen or change the culture.

No hugging required
But where do you start if you want to change your culture? The prospect of bringing about cultural change in any organisation is daunting, particularly in those which have existed for some time and where the culture is well-established. And by the way, don't be fooled into thinking that weak cultures are less well-established and therefore easier to change than strong cultures. On the contrary, they can be even more difficult to change, because people are not aligned and are used to getting away with breaking the rules. Besides, people who are used to a weak culture may find the cult-like nature of a strong culture rather daunting if they don't wholeheartedly buy into its values.

Culture change is a slow and complex process, and many companies have failed to bring about anything beyond the most superficial changes. Initiatives often fail because of lack of clarity, both about what needs to change and how to bring that change about. When it comes to implementing culture change, people are frequently at a loss about what to do. Many organisations plump for the 'spray-and-pray' approach: they release a barrage of communications – posters, screen savers, cards to be placed in top pockets – and then pray that it will all sink in somehow. Another approach is the 'sheep-dip' (not a technical term). This involves taking large groups of people (middle managers usually get picked on first) through mass training events, in the hope that they will emerge at the other end as believers, having rid themselves of all their bad behaviours. Such approaches may be used to *contribute* to a culture change programme, but there is no doubt that in themselves they are not enough. The effects are short-lived, and, because of their superficial nature, they tend to be greeted with scepticism by employees.

Some organisations abandon the spray-and-pray and sheep-dip approaches in favour of more adventurous methods. This is not always a good thing. I have been astonished by the bizarre activities in which some have engaged. One example I heard of was a company which was trying to make its culture more dynamic. They sent groups of their senior managers on a course where they were encouraged to step out of their comfort zones. To facilitate this, one man ended up having to *wash another guy's feet*. Another organisation took groups of managers through a weird event where everyone had to openly declare their greatest hang-ups, preferably bursting into tears in the process. They justified this approach using *the principles of quantum mechanics*. I was a physicist in a former career, and certainly the study of quantum mechanics might lead you to burst into tears, but I fail to see its connection with culture change.

A key aspect of culture is the way business relationships are handled – relationships between staff and customers, and amongst members of staff. This is especially true of professional service companies like KPMG, whose main resource is people. But culture initiatives do not focus on touchy feely relationship issues like feelings and loyalty. They focus instead on the formal, professional aspects of people relationships: commitment, integrity, and a dedication to quality.

Thankfully, most organisations don't engage in such extreme

acts of ritual humiliation. Still, many managers associate culture change with more mundane, but nonetheless cringing, experiences gained through 'touchy feely' team-building activities. As one macho KPMG male put it to me, 'I hope we don't have to go off into the woods and hug each other.' Tempted as I was to say 'No, but you might want to ask that big guy over there if he'll hold your hand', I assured him that group hugs weren't on the agenda.

Many companies don't even get to the stage of undertaking any activity, however superficial, because another pitfall of culture change is that it can quickly degenerate into a talking shop. Before you know it, you will have spent a year running endless group meetings, where people discuss a multitude of wrongs (apart from what is wrong with themselves, of course) without making any attempt at looking for solutions. Such groups can produce an impressive number of flipcharts, mostly headed 'issues' and rarely headed 'actions'. In other words, by spending so much time talking, they skilfully avoid having to *do* anything to change the status quo. Of course it is constructive to get issues on the table, just as it is important to allow people to vent their frustrations. But if the record gets stuck at this point, it can cause damage to the organisation by generating too much negativity and a feeling of helplessness in the face of seemingly insurmountable problems. Sure, a group whinge can be very therapeutic, but if it gets out of hand people can end up feeling miserable and not much else. Colin coined the term 'MBS' (Monumental Bitching Session) for such phenomena, and this does convey pretty well the nature of the beast. Anyone managing a process like this needs to be able to move the discussion on to solutions, and to keep the group in a positive frame of mind.

All in all, it is easy to see why any pragmatic businessperson could get turned off by culture change. It is still filed alongside astrology and black magic in the mind of the average business manager, and it really is time that some of the mystery was taken out of it. It's hard, but it's not rocket science. And there really are some practical, pragmatic actions which can be taken to bring about a lasting shift in culture. So now we have talked about what *isn't* the path to culture change, let's reflect for a minute on what it *is*.

The path to culture change

Corporate culture is a living, changing system which operates at four levels. It is easy to make changes to the most superficial level, but such changes can be purely cosmetic and short-lived. At the deepest level, we find the core values of the culture. These are very difficult to change and respond only slowly to long-term shifts in the other levels of the culture. To achieve lasting change it is essential to understand and work with core values. Because core values are very deeply held and practically unconscious beliefs, they are not immediately accessible to people trying to identify them. Without the right approach, it is hard to get to the core of culture. This is why so many culture change programmes fall victim to the type of activity described above. This book gives details of a framework and a process which can be used to get to the heart of culture. At the highest level (described below), the process is very simple. Its beauty is that it can be adapted to suit the complexities of every individual organisation.

Before embarking on any process of culture change, you need to understand thoroughly what you are dealing with. In other words, you need an in-depth understanding of the principles of corporate culture – how it manifests itself, how it is structured, and how it changes. The following chapter offers a clear model for how culture works in an organisation, and, based on this, what can be done to change it.

You use this model to gain a deep understanding of your existing corporate culture. This is the initial step on the path to culture change. Like any other journey, it is essential to know where you are starting from. Only when you know where you are, can you decide where you need to go and how best to get there. And the chances are that when you study your existing culture in depth, you will find that there are many things about it that you want to preserve or strengthen.

The second step is to define the culture which you wish to have. This involves defining the set of values to which the organisation aspires, and determining how the other levels of the culture can be aligned with these values. A rich picture of the desired culture is painted, which helps people to imagine what it will look and feel like in real life.

Having established clearly the current situation and the desired culture, all that remains is to take the steps necessary to shift from one to the other. In brief, people need to learn to live according to the new values. They need to demonstrate them through their behaviour. At the same time, the new values need to be reflected in the day-to-day processes, systems and work environment. Implementation therefore focuses on making the behavioural and organisational changes necessary to bring the aspired values to life.

Because culture is integral to the daily life of the organisation, the culture change effort should fit in as much as possible with the ongoing activities of the organisation. Out-of-the-ordinary or bizarre events such as those described in the previous section can be harmful, because they alienate the culture change process from the normal organisational programme (not to mention giving it the reputation for being something freaky). Culture change should permeate all aspects of the company, and because culture is a living system, any process of change which is naturally evolving rather than radical is more likely to succeed.

Later chapters of this book give a rigorous framework for understanding and changing culture. The path to culture change which we took at KPMG is described in depth to illustrate the points made and show how the methods work in practice. KPMG is a global organisation with over 100,000 people. The challenges in aligning the culture of such a diverse organisation were many. The theory behind our thinking, the process we used and the real-life experiences we gained in three years of effort to revitalise the firm's culture are presented in the following chapters. Many of the lessons we have learned at KPMG and the approaches we have taken can be used in a wider context to the benefit of anyone seeking to bring about culture change in their own organisation, be it large or small, public sector or in the business world.

Chapter 2

THE PRINCIPLES OF CULTURE CHANGE

'Please leave your values at the front desk'
(Notice in a Parisian hotel foyer)

Ask a group of employees to describe their company culture and you will be bombarded with all sorts of verbiage: disparate adjectives, slogans, popular management jargon, anecdotes, grievances. Ask them to describe their ideal culture and you will end up with a similar assortment (minus the grievances, naturally, but with a few extra, lofty wishes added). The chances are that not much of what you will hear will help you pin down what it really is that needs to change, never mind how those changes could be accomplished.

People find it difficult to define culture, because everyone has a different concept of what it constitutes. Many have their own, favourite definitions, so when it comes to describing culture, the scope for misunderstanding is huge. You really need to be precise in your explanations. Waving your hands around and getting philosophical won't help. To be able to talk in an authoritative way about culture, you will need a clear framework or model.

This chapter begins by presenting a framework to describe organisational culture. (This was perhaps the most useful piece of theory I used in the early stages of KPMG's culture change process.) Subsequent sections explain how the framework can be used to understand more deeply the nature of organisational culture, and how it can be applied to culture change. Applying basic principles to culture change initiatives will then be described, including approaches to developing an appropriate strategy, and a high-level process.

A framework for understanding culture

There was a bit of a craze for inventing culture models a few years ago, so there is no shortage. Unfortunately many of them will not be particularly helpful to you. Many models propose generic cultural types invented from goodness knows where. In general, these won't get you any further in your understanding of your own culture or what needs to change. You might be able to say, as one client of mine once did: 'We had a study done and we have an *Apollo* culture – highly formal and highly centrally directed.' Well, so what? I suppose 'Apollo', being a Greek god and by all accounts a big hunk, sounds better than 'control freak'. But it doesn't exactly paint a rich picture of the organisation (how much did they pay for the study, I wonder?). A model is no use unless it can help you describe in graphic detail the culture which is under scrutiny.

Pragmatism is essential when it comes to choosing which model to use. The model needs to be rigorous, that is, based on some sort of reliable research. It has to be adaptable and applicable to your own situation. Simplicity is also a blessing. My advice is to steer clear of anything which appears very rigid, because no culture can be fitted into a straitjacket definition. Any model which proposes generic cultural types should, in my opinion, be avoided, because each culture is unique and deserves to be described in its own right. Deep suspicion of any model using a two-by-two matrix is also healthy, because such models will, by their very nature, only describe two dimensions of a culture. Notwithstanding the fact that these might be two dimensions which your culture doesn't even have, I'm sure it's more complex than that.

We used something which is not a fixed model but a general framework, which we were then able to populate with descriptions of our own culture. The framework is very simple: it is the descriptions of our own, unique characteristics which enable it to reflect the complexities of our culture. It is based on a model proposed by the brilliant Edgar Schein (*Organisational Culture and Leadership*, 1992), and describes culture as having distinct, interacting levels.

Schein is one of the grandfathers of the science of organisations. He approaches corporate culture like an anthropologist, and his theories draw heavily on his research into organisational psychology and group learning. From his model we can see how the different elements of culture are linked, as well as seeing how they arise. We also gain an appreciation of which elements of culture can and cannot be easily changed. Unlike many of his contemporaries, his framework does not presuppose any generic cultural types. Instead, it gives us a structure which can be applied to any culture. The application of his framework helps us to classify and understand the unique characteristics of the culture which we are studying.

At KPMG we adapted Schein's framework only a little for our own use. In our version, we define culture as having four distinct *levels*: artefacts, behaviours, espoused values and core values. In Schein's original model, behaviours and artefacts are combined in one level. For reasons which will become apparent, we found that it was more useful for our purposes to separate these into two distinct levels. We also refer to the deepest level of the culture as 'core values', whereas Schein labels these 'assumptions'. Essentially we are talking about the same thing, but we did find that Collins and Porras's thinking on core ideology (*Built to Last*, 3rd edition, Random House Business Books, 2000) added to Schein's original definition of what we find at the core of culture. When we had finished with definitions, we drew up our framework in a diagram which looks like a target. It is reproduced in Figure 2.1.

The framework was invaluable when it came to establishing consistent definitions. Not only did it help us explain to people what we meant, it also helped us establish what can and cannot be changed about culture. We found that when people understood the framework, they were able to give us focused feedback which was easy to interpret. This is a far cry from the widely varied responses which are usually given to questions about culture.

The innermost circle represents the core of the culture, which is also the level at which culture is *unconscious*. The outermost levels

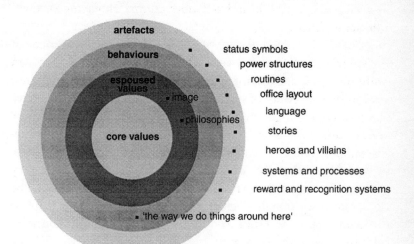

Figure 2.1: *A framework for understanding culture*

are much more easily observed and are part of the *conscious* processes in the organisation. The deeper you go into the core, the more unconscious or taken-for-granted the cultural processes become. To elaborate on this, let's look in a little more detail at the four levels:

Artefacts
This is culture at its most superficial level. Artefacts are the things we can observe and feel in the work environment, for example, typical symbols of the culture, organisational structures, rules, processes and routines, as well as more mundane things like the office layout and the way people dress for work. Artefacts also include what gets talked about – who are the company heroes, or more interestingly, the villains? What 'taboos' and 'war stories' are talked about at the coffee machine? All these things exist for a reason, and they have their roots in the deeper elements of the culture.

It is often fun to study artefacts, and there are a few interesting frameworks to help you classify them, one of the more useful being

Johnson's 'cultural web' ('Managing Strategic Change – Strategy, Culture and Action', 1992). Artefacts are easy to observe because they are very visible. They are right there at the forefront of every employee's consciousness and are manifested in the physical environment. They are easy to spot, even for an outsider.

However, a study of superficial things only leads to superficial understanding. It is very unwise to pass judgement on an organisation's culture on the basis of artefacts alone. Organisations which have similar-looking artefacts might nevertheless be driven by very different systems of values. For example, suppose you were to observe an organisation where staff had to clock in on arrival and clock out when they left. How authoritarian, you might think – they don't trust their staff to do a full day's work. This could be true. But there are many other plausible reasons – maybe it is an organisation where security is important, and where it is vital to know exactly who is in the building and when. Maybe it has something to do with production systems, or local health-and-safety regulations – who knows what values system underpins this artefact? You won't, unless you delve further into the inner layers of the culture.

Behaviours

At the next deepest level of culture we find ingrained patterns or 'norms' of behaviour. Every new joiner in an organisation quickly learns about 'the way we do things around here'. These are the codes of practice which get you through the day, which define what you need to do to 'get on' and warn you of 'career-limiting moves' to be avoided. If you are lucky, the 'official' codes of practice will match reality, but more often than not, it is the unwritten rules of behaviour which are important.

Behavioural norms are not as obvious as artefacts to the observer, but nor are they buried completely in the unconscious processes of the organisation. It is still easy to find out about them. Behaviour is driven by the accepted values in the organisation. The identification of behavioural norms and their causes is key to understanding which values are at the heart of the company culture.

Espoused values
These are the values which an organisation claims to hold, or temporarily promotes to suit a business need. Espoused values may be used to influence behaviour if they are being promoted seriously as part of a culture change programme. However, many organisations suffer from a common complaint called 'poster syndrome'. That is, they invent a new set of values, distribute designer posters, mouse mats or screen savers proclaiming these values, and then wonder why nothing has changed. It goes without saying that a set of values will not have any influence on the organisation's culture if they are espoused but not practised. Some individual instances of behaviour may successfully be altered in reference to espoused values, but generally speaking, no matter how good the intention, behaviours tend to revert to the norms dictated by the true or 'core' values. If no serious work is done to make espoused values a reality, they will never become any more than a poster phenomenon.

Core values
These are the unconscious, taken-for-granted beliefs, perceptions, thoughts and assumptions at the heart of the organisation's culture. Core values are the timeless guiding principles for behaviour, decisions and actions. If in some strange circumstances, continuing to do business meant compromising the core values, people in the organisation would choose to change the nature of the business rather than change the values.

The source of all elements of the culture lies at this deepest level. Everything we see at the outer levels of culture – artefacts, behaviours, and even espoused values – derives from the core values.

Core values become ingrained over time. They are 'second nature' – acted upon without even being thought about. While a few companies have written-down statements of values which reflect accurately what is at the heart of their culture, in many organisations core values remain unconscious, so they are difficult to articulate or identify directly.

Core values are small in number – usually between three and

five. They represent the few, fundamental ideals which the organisation will never give up.

How do you know when you have the 'right' values?
In the last chapter, we talked about the considerable benefits which a strong culture can bring to business performance. But how do you know which are the best values for your business? Most pragmatic people would want to be pretty certain, before they embarked on a process of culture change, that they were moving towards the right ones.

In spite of what you might think, all the research into organisational culture shows that it doesn't really matter so much what the values statement *says*. The 'right' values are those which are truly believed, shared and put into practice by the people in the organisation. Some of the world's most successful organisations have values statements which, to the untrained eye, would appear to be missing a few essential ingredients. For example, Sony doesn't mention its customers at all in its values statement. Nordstrom, surely a business in which people are fundamental to success, does not reflect this in its creed. However, no one can deny that these are both successful organisations which are very clear about what they *do* stand for. What makes the difference with these companies is not what their values say, but the fact that they are the basis of a very strong culture.

In other words, there is no such thing as an 'expedient' set of values. One CEO can't look at another and say 'our values are better than yours'. For a culture to be strong, the values need to reflect what is truly believed by the people in the organisation. They need to be intrinsic to the company, not designed to perfection to cover every eventuality. It is better to have a simple statement of values in which everyone believes than a slick, engineered version which never gets off the poster. Many organisations waste time in wordsmithing, when what they really need to do is engage people's hearts and minds.

Understanding your culture, warts-and-all
Anyone wishing to lead or effectively manage an organisation, or

anyone about to embark on a process of culture change, needs to understand very well the culture within which they are currently operating. The model presented above is a good starting point for diagnosing an existing culture.

The culture framework is very similar to the models of personality we use when describing individuals. Therefore, if we think about how a person might be analysed, we can see that we could analyse an organisation's culture in the same way.

When we first meet a person, we all make snap judgements on appearances, speech and mannerisms. However, very few of us (except those unusually blessed people who claim to be 'good judges of character') would presume to have an insight into that person's deeper personality and values based only on these observations. Likewise, in diagnosing an organisation's culture, examining the artefacts alone will not tell you very much about what underpins them. You need to look below the surface.

On the other hand, even the most naïve amateur psychologist wouldn't expect a valid answer to the question: 'What are your deep personality traits and values?' These things, being unconscious, are difficult to articulate for all but the most self-aware individuals. Likewise, in most organisations, people will have difficulty articulating the core values of the culture, because these too are deeply buried in their collective unconscious.

With an individual, analysing behaviour patterns and determining their source is a key to identifying deeper personality traits. We can apply the same principle in diagnosing an organisation's culture. An organisation's core values can be identified by first examining patterns of behaviour, and then finding out what causes them. Behaviour is the key to gaining a deep understanding of the underlying traits of an organisation's culture.

Finding the keys to values: Identifying behavioural norms
Behavioural norms are key to understanding the core values of culture – but where do you start if you want to identify behavioural norms?

You have two choices: you can either adopt a quantitative

approach, which means using survey techniques and asking people to score questionnaires, or you can approach it in a more qualitative way by talking to people, gathering opinions and asking them to comment on their experiences. (There is a third choice, of course, which is to combine both methods.)

If you choose to use survey techniques, you may find designing your questionnaire quite a challenge. Deciding which questions to ask is more difficult than it appears. If you are designing a survey to research behavioural norms in your organisation, you will need a fairly in-depth understanding of the culture to know what to ask about in the first place. You may find yourself having to run focus groups and interviews (in other words, having to employ more qualitative methods) to get the information you need. (In which case – why not just go straight to using qualitative methods?) In addition, questionnaire design is a science in itself: you need clear, unambiguous questions, you need to avoid leading the respondent in any way, to understand how people react when asked to give scored responses, and to make sure that your design will deliver meaningful data. Questionnaire design is not so difficult if you are asking about factual data – for example, it would be easy to draw up a questionnaire to find out how many white males between the ages of 20 and 35 in North London possess mobile phones, but where 'softer' issues such as culture are concerned it is not such a straightforward exercise.

Of course you may decide not to design your own questionnaire – there are many well-researched, proprietary culture surveys on the market which can help you in identifying behaviour patterns. I have had a fair amount of experience using such things, and used in the right circumstances, some can be very effective. Most culture surveys come in the form of multiple-choice questionnaires which measure the degree to which pre-defined, generic behavioural styles are present in the organisation. These have the benefit of being quick to score and the results are usually easy to compare across divisions or demographic groups, and in some cases with external data.

However, before you rush off and buy thousands of copies of the latest survey, bear in mind that like most things generic, proprietary surveys have limitations, especially when it comes to describing something as complex as culture. I'll give you an example from my own experience:

In some parts of KPMG we made extensive use of proprietary culture surveys, particularly in the early stages of the culture change process. Although we used reputable suppliers and well-validated tools, I always had nagging doubts: how could a questionnaire which measured pre-defined, generic behavioural styles describe fully our own peculiarities and quirks? Why did the survey measure only twelve behavioural styles and not thirteen? Why not one hundred styles? After using the survey, we ended up with a rough impression of dominant behaviours in KPMG, but when we tried to use it as a basis for discovering what our underlying values might be, we found that it was not accurate enough.

Not surprisingly, identifying behavioural norms is not as simple as the questionnaires make out. You can never get a complete picture from such surveys. Any survey which measures generic behavioural styles is, just by virtue of being 'one size fits all', too crude. It is like trying to paint a Constable landscape with a decorating brush. I remember as a child that there was a TV programme where Rolf Harris, an Australian entertainer, used to do just this. In those days, when I didn't know a thing about art, I thought he was a genius. But I wouldn't want one of his works to hang in my living room today. So what does this tell us about surveys? You cannot get a rich picture of the culture using a broad-brush approach.

Another danger of relying solely on quantitative techniques is a common complaint which I term 'survey addiction'. It is easy to get carried away with the idea of surveying culture. Measuring becomes an end in itself, and people can become obsessed with the scores obtained, losing sight of the real issues. To give an example, I once had a client in the banking sector who used a very powerful proprietary culture survey to measure their behavioural norms. They took their (atrocious) results very seriously, which was good. But when I asked one of their directors to define his goals for culture change, he gave me a puzzled look and exclaimed, 'To improve these scores of course!' Hmmm. He went on to explain that he had issued a remit that the survey would be repeated every six months. I expressed a concern that this was excessive, pointing out that because culture is slow to change, they were unlikely to see much improvement after six months. Not only would this be disappointing and bad for morale, but maybe the time and effort they would devote to conducting the survey could be better spent in other culture-changing activities.

Don't be put off altogether – proprietary surveys can be useful as *part* of culture diagnosis, particularly in the initial stages when you need to get a general sense of what is going on. Appropriate use of standard culture surveys can significantly help the process of diagnosis. But in truth, the only way to get a complete picture about behaviour in organisations is to listen to people talk about it. Qualitative techniques must be included in the diagnostic process. At KPMG, we ran numerous interviews and focus groups to give us good, qualitative feedback on the types of behaviour which prevailed in our culture. We devised a number of methods for finding out about 'the way we do things around here' (these will be described later). We listened and probed and in the end, arrived at a very clear, warts-and-all picture of the firm's unique behaviour patterns.

The values behind the behaviours: Using behavioural norms to find out about values

If you have established what the behaviour patterns are in an organisation, you will be in a position to delve further down into the heart of the culture to find out what values and beliefs are causing them. At KPMG we did this in focus groups and interviews by employing an iterative investigative approach – which in plain English means that in the irritating manner of small children, we asked *why* we do things the way we do and kept asking 'why' until we had arrived at what seemed like an underlying value. (Miraculously, no one lost his temper and said 'because Daddy says so'.)

Using this technique, it is possible to peel back the layers of behaviours and find the values which underpin them. However, any list of values which you derive from behaviour patterns in this way will probably need further refinement before you can be sure that you have arrived at your organisation's small number of core values. At KPMG we applied the tests suggested by Collins and Porras (*Built to Last*, 3rd edition, Random House Business Books, 2000) to identify which of our 'unedited' list of values were truly core. For example, taking each proposed value in turn we posed the question that if the world changed and it was no longer helpful to our business to hold this value, would we be prepared to change what we do so that we could keep it as a value, or would we rather just forget about it? We were trying to establish which of the values KPMG believed in most passionately. We were looking for abhorrent reactions at the prospect of abandoning a particular value – this would convince us that it was truly core. In the same way, you will need to find out from people 'what they would lie under a train for'. (When you look at it like this, it is not surprising that such core values are small in number!)

In order to plan a route for your culture change, you need to know where you're starting from. So the first thing to do is to understand thoroughly the nature of your existing culture – for example, how you and other people typically behave, what values genuinely drive that behaviour, how people actually get ahead in the organisation, and what kind of example is set by the leaders. The credibility of your culture change programme depends on the honesty with which you draw this picture.

As a first step, you need to be able to see yourself as others see you. This means asking for feedback about your part of the organisation, your team – and yourself.

When you feel you have arrived at a set of core values for your organisation, it is worth double-checking that you have got it right. You can validate what you found by backtracking and looking for evidence of these values at the other levels of culture. How do you see these values reflected in behaviours and artefacts? The outer levels of the culture should all hold evidence for the values at the core. At KPMG we took the culture framework and, for each value at the core, plotted on the diagram the examples of image and philosophies, behavioural patterns and artefacts of culture which were manifestations of that value. This helped not only in validating our findings about core values, but also in understanding better what the implications of changing parts of our culture might be.

How culture can be changed

The framework helps us see which constituents of culture we can change, and the effect such changes might have on other aspects of the culture. Some elements of culture are easy to modify while others are slow or nearly impossible to change directly. Changes at some levels will lead to long-lasting shifts in the culture, while those at other levels will have only the most superficial effects. We examine this in more detail below, taking each level of culture in turn.

Scratching the surface: changing artefacts

Just as an individual can easily alter personal 'artefacts' with different clothes and a haircut, it is easy to change the artefacts of an organisation's culture. Some artefacts are symbolic of the culture, and getting rid of them can send a strong signal that there is commitment to change. Likewise, replacing a particular artefact with something strikingly different can send a very powerful message.

However, changing artefacts does not always produce such dramatic results. Here is an example from KPMG. Many years ago in some parts of the firm we had separate dining facilities for partners. This was a long-outdated, special privilege which was removed in order to demonstrate a commitment to bringing partners closer to staff. At the time, this was no doubt a grand gesture. The problem was, that a few months later, the gesture was forgotten. Especially since a large number of the partners still did not grace the communal sandwich bar with their presence. Instead, they upheld the old culture by sending their secretaries out on a mission to bring back food which they later consumed in the comfort of their offices!

Anyone undertaking culture change should bear in mind that

changing artefacts alone is not enough to bring about a lasting shift in culture. The benefits gained will be short-lived. If this is so, you might say, 'why bother'? Unfortunately, you have no choice. While changing artefacts does not usually bring great benefits, *not* changing them causes a disproportionate amount of damage to a culture programme. So, for example, if you redesign your performance management systems to reflect your new corporate values, this alone is unlikely to make a radical difference to your organisation. People will not exclaim joyfully, 'Look how serious this culture change is – they have changed the performance management system!'. But if you leave things as they are, they will say, 'Well, the new culture certainly can't be that important – they haven't even changed the performance management system.' There is a law of physics which says 'to every action there is an equal reaction'. Unfortunately it does not seem to apply to human nature.

Going deeper: changing behaviour

Behaviours are more deeply ingrained in the culture than artefacts and, not surprisingly, implementing behaviour change leads to longer-lasting shifts in culture.

Changing behaviour is not easy and requires absolute commitment, particularly from leadership who, as the role models for the rest of the people in the organisation, will probably need to change first. Leaders also have the responsibility for making decisions about the people (and therefore, types of behaviour) they wish to promote. So they really need to buy into the new 'way we do things around here'.

Behaviour change requires focused initiatives and a high degree of sensitivity, patience and persistence. However, if people can change the way they think about things, if they can see a good reason to change their behaviour, and if they are provided with practical support, behaviour change is possible.

Espoused values: from poster to reality

On the face of it, espoused values are easy to change – you just write a new set when you feel like it! Needless to say, that won't make any difference unless what you espouse is truly brought to life. Espoused values – what you *claim* to believe in, and the images, goals and philosophies which you put in place to support them, need to be truly derived from the core values your organisation has (or would like to have), and be actively used to promote desired changes to behaviours or artefacts. Care needs to be taken. Superficiality needs to be banished, and the temptation to chop and change espoused values at will should be avoided at all costs. Otherwise you will end up with just so much lip-service and meaningless slogans on posters.

In KPMG we were fanatical about not making our values a poster phenomenon. We're not saying that the values *shouldn't* appear on a poster, but unless people see commitment and, more importantly, *actions* to make them a reality, a poster can become a license to generate cynicism.

The heart of the matter: core values

Core values are the essence of culture and there has always been a debate about whether or not they can be changed at all. They are certainly slow and almost impossible to change directly, particularly in a mature organisation where they have been reinforced over a long period of time. To achieve a lasting shift at this level, the desired values need to be learned and the old values need to be 'unlearned'. People will have to see evidence to be convinced. In other words, the new values have to be tested over and over again in day-to-day situations, and lead to successful outcomes, before they are accepted in the culture. By the same token, the application of the 'old' values has to be seen to lead repeatedly to failure.

One thing you can be sure of: changing core values will be very, very *slow*. It would take an age for a new set of values to evolve into the unconscious beliefs on which people base their behaviour at work. Likewise, an organisation will be slow to rid itself of the values it wishes to discard. However, how often would an organisation really seek to abandon one set of values in favour of another? Any organisation which wishes to adopt a radically different set of values needs to be asked: If the present culture is so

> It's clear that the more visible aspects of company culture are susceptible to change or influence. We assume, but don't really know from experience, whether the deepest level of culture – core values – can also change. In the case of KPMG, from what I've seen so far, I'm optimistic that it can. The important thing is to believe in change, and not to let the laggards set the agenda. It's always easier not to change – but then you can soon find that the organisation is out of step with the rest of the business world and it's too late.

deplorable, why not just shut down and start again? For most organisations, and certainly in our own experience at KPMG, radical changes are not necessary. It is important not to throw away the baby with the bath water. It is better to look long and hard at the present culture, to appreciate the good in the existing values, but also look at where they may be limiting the organisation. Then it can be decided what needs to be added, and what taken away from the existing system to define the desired culture. It should not be a case of gung-ho 'out with the old, in with the new!'. Not only is this impossible, it's likely to be unnecessary.

Focus on what you can *change*
In summary, it is easy to change cultural artefacts, although this alone will not bring about lasting culture change. It is harder, but not impossible, to change behaviour, and the benefits of this are more long-lasting. Espoused values are easily altered, but this will have no effect unless some serious effort is put into making them come alive. Core values are slow to shift and, because they are so deeply ingrained in the organisation's unconscious, cannot be changed directly.

Where does this leave us if we want to bring about culture change?

The answer is simple – focus on changing what you can and let the things you can't change look after themselves. It is possible to change artefacts and behaviour, so this is where to start. However, these changes need to have some direction and your desired set of values will guide you in this. Your aim will be to continually reinforce the new values through changes to artefacts and behaviour. If you do this, the new values will eventually come to be 'learned' by the organisation, and in the longer term will become core to the new culture.

Therefore, when it comes to implementing your desired culture, you should aim to:

- Align *artefacts* with the values of your desired culture by making organisational changes, e.g. to processes, systems, rewards and recognition, power structures, communications etc.
- Ensure that the *behaviours* which support your desired values become the norm, by running *behaviour change* initiatives and personal development activities.

There is a further piece of advice, based on our experience at KPMG: throughout the firm's culture change process, we always made it clear that our published values statement represented our *aspirations* – we acknowledged freely that these values were not yet a reality. We did this because we knew that core values do not change overnight and we did not want to invoke a cynical response. What we did say was that we passionately believed in our aspired values, and that we would be using them as our guide as we set out on the path to more lasting culture change.

The good thing about being on the path is that there are benefits along the way.

Culture change in context
By now we have the beginnings of a recipe for culture change. Or do we?

I am a keen cook, but whenever I follow a recipe exactly, I often have disastrous results. Why is this? Maybe it's because I can't replicate the conditions of a top restaurant. Also, if I am aiming to accommodate my own tastes and those of my guests, I know I will have to alter the ingredients here and there. So it is with culture change. There is no one authoritative recipe which can tell you exactly how to do it. Of course there are some general principles which you can follow. But to bring about successful culture change, you will need to develop an approach which is specially suited to your own organisation. This will require you to do two things:

- Firstly, you will need to understand the environment in which you are working: its dynamics, its limitations and its opportunities
- Secondly, you will have to consider the end result: what is the nature of the change you are trying to bring about?

Understanding the dynamics

Regarding the first point: I have often encountered, both with my clients and within KPMG, a naïve belief that emulating the actions of some great organisation will be a formula for success. How often have I heard business icons such as Jack Welch quoted, or Percy Barnevik's ideas held up as the perfect solution? More times than I care to recall. These people are exemplary leaders and have deservedly achieved great fame. They clearly understood exactly what would and would not work in their own organisations. However, there is no guarantee that their recipe for success will work in *your* organisation! Each company has its own set of peculiarities, subtleties and unwritten rules. These will be mainly cultural, but will also be affected by structure, governance, the business environment and other factors. Before starting any major change process, it is vital that time is spent on truly understanding how the organisation works, and considering how this should be taken into account in the approach.

This is where insiders in the organisation have a huge advantage over outsiders such as external consultants. Insiders will be familiar with the management style and the language used. They will know the politics: what has worked in the past and what has failed. They will know who is important, which tone to adopt, how decisions are made, what to include and what to leave out. They will know when to push, when to try out new and different things, and when to go with the flow. They may not know all these things consciously, in which case an outsider can help them articulate, but they will know them all the same. Time needs to be spent reflecting, drawing out ideas and talking to the organisation's experienced, successful leaders.

The nature of the change

The second thing you need to think about is the nature of the change which you are aiming to bring about. Is it a major change? Is it radical? Whom will it affect? What are its aims?

The management style adopted when carrying out any initiatives should be in keeping with the end-goals of the change. For example, suppose you were trying to increase two-way communications in your company. You would look ridiculous if you tried to promote this using one-way communications systems such as videos and mass presentations. Your approach would need to reflect the very thing you were trying to bring about. To be consistent with your end-goal you might try running discussion groups, or using media such as e-mail to enable people to reply.

A strategy for culture change

Both these factors: the dynamics of the organisation and the nature of the change, are important in developing a strategy for culture change. Perhaps the best way to illustrate what we mean is to give examples from KPMG, and show how we took both into account in planning our overall approach.

KPMG's strategy for culture change Part I: The firm's dynamics

Life would have been so easy if we had been able to consult with KPMG's International Board, draw up a set of values and issue these to the firm's practices throughout the world. We could then sit back while delighted staff all over the globe embraced the new culture. Our only dilemma would be how best to monitor the business benefits as they rolled in. Well, I can dream.

Of course KPMG does not work like this. But how does it work? This was the question facing us as we set out on the path to culture change. It is vital to figure this out. Knowing what opportunities to use and where to intervene, when to push, when to back off and when to let go, is the key to the success of any change process – unfortunately it can't be found in a textbook.

The best way to understand an organisation's dynamics is to listen to the people who know the company best. It is a little like conducting research into history: you need to find out from people about what happened in the company's past and why. How were major changes implemented? What succeeded and failed? It is also worth looking at how the company is governed – what are the accepted management practices, the lines of authority, formal and informal? What general characteristics do people seem to have in common? How does this affect how things get done? What is valued? Who is listened to? All this needs to be found out in building a picture of how the company works. As an insider, you might know a lot of this already and it is mainly a matter of ordering your thoughts. As an outsider, you will have a lot of asking to do. At KPMG we had the benefit, in our team, of more years in the firm than we cared to admit. Colin in particular had over thirty years' experience of KPMG's quirks and intuitively knew what would and would not work. The following paragraphs give some of the insights into KPMG which helped us in formulating our strategy for culture change.

In understanding KPMG's dynamics, the first thing that needs to be appreciated is that the firm is a partnership. So, unlike most corporate structures, the partners not only manage the business, they also *own* the business. With over 7,000 partners worldwide, the traditional concept of partnership has lost its meaning somewhat, but nevertheless, much of the partnership ethos remains. In examining what makes the firm 'tick', we can trace a lot back to the partnership model.

The benefit of a partnership culture is that people operate with a great deal of autonomy and entrepreneurship – partners feel and act as if they are running their own businesses. The disadvantage is that people operate with a great deal of autonomy and entrepreneurship – partners feel and act as if they are running their own businesses. In other words, while autonomy is great for motivation and creativity, it also has a downside. People have a habit of doing things in their own way and often comply with central policy only if they feel like it. The distribution of authority is opaque, coercion doesn't work and generally speaking, persuasion is the best currency. Consensus (if you can get it) is the preferred method of decision-making.

Another relic of the partnership culture is the division between partners and the rest of the people (referred to as 'staff') in the firm. This can go quite deep. For example, one young partner once complained to me that our values didn't appear to apply to partners. I was more than a little surprised. When I asked why not, I was told 'Well, the values statement only talks about our *people*, not about partners'. I pointed out that, with a few notable exceptions, partners mostly belonged to the human race too. On the surface, this sounds like another amusing anecdote, but there is actually a very important point here. The partnership *is* separate from the rest of KPMG's people in that it is a special group with special power. It is the one group in the firm whose buy-in to any change is an absolute necessity. Partners have power, voting rights and a leadership role. Because of this, a lot of effort needs to be directed towards engaging this group. This is particularly true when undertaking behavioural change, because the partners are role models and as such, comprise the group which probably has to change most.

> Before the culture change programme, KPMG had very clearly defined hierarchies. Associated with these were unwritten rules and an established pecking order. The partners, for instance, would never have dreamt of asking a non-partner for feedback about their personal performance; only the views of another, more senior partner would be of interest. Conversely, any partner would feel entitled to pass judgement on a member of 'staff', as non-partners were known. We particularly wanted to avoid elitist attitudes like this in our new culture.

Not everyone would agree with me on this. For example, I was talking to an external consultant once about how we were bringing about behavioural change in the firm. She was concerned that partners were much more heavily involved than staff. She turned up her nose and commented that the process looked quite '*top-down*', as if this was a dirty word. Well, the reality is, if our junior auditors want to bring about behavioural change and the partners don't like it, the partnership will stop it. But if the partners want to bring about behavioural change and the audit juniors don't like it, that's just tough on the audit juniors. I'm an idealist and a democrat and I don't like it either, but we have to work in the real world here! Leadership role modelling is a top-down kind of thing. We did think this through (the fact that clients can think is something which that particular consultant appeared to overlook), and we focused on engaging the stakeholder group that would have most leverage – the group that we could not afford *not* to engage. However, I will concede that every organisation is different and a predominantly top-down approach might not be good everywhere. What you need to do is understand thoroughly the power, influence and potential resistance of key stakeholder groups, and their sensitivity to your particular change. Then you can decide whether your approach is top-down, bottom-up, whole-system or whatever the latest thinking is.

Of course there are other factors besides the partnership structure which contribute to KPMG's dynamics. The firm has a diverse mix of national cultures. Unlike our competitors and many other global organisations, we are not dominated by our American practice. In fact, we are not dominated by *any* one of our national practices – we are truly multinational. We do not have one leader and many followers. Even if we wanted to, we could not direct our global organisation out of any one country, as this would lead to multiple rebellions and defections by all the other national practices. We are closer than any of our competitors to being a true 'world enterprise', that is, a company which embraces many national cultures. This is our unique strength and our great opportunity. It is also a significant source of struggle – let's face it, a mono-culture is less diverse and less interesting, but it's easier to manage. We would be lying if we said we never looked with a twinge of envy at the ease with which some of our competitors have issued directives from their US headquarters and watched them get implemented straight away, all over the globe. Anything we do has to demonstrate a sensitivity to local culture and be responsive to the needs of our local clients and employees. There will always be a tension in balancing global and local interests, but at least we all share the belief that it is the right thing to do.

Another of KPMG's peculiarities is that the firm probably invented the 'not invented here syndrome'. Otherwise it wouldn't have caught on as much as it has. Our people like to do things in their own way, and then argue about whose way is best. (These arguments can be especially fierce and entertaining when the two proposed solutions are practically identical.) We have, in the past, incurred considerable costs through duplication of effort. In more recent years, we have become more pragmatic and less precious, but nonetheless, our people are much more ready to accept solutions if they have been party to their development. The result is that in running an international initiative, if you want to avoid resistance to things not invented 'here', then you have to make 'here' very big – in other words, the whole worldwide firm needs to have a say.

Who is listened to in the organisation? In KPMG, to have an opinion that really matters, you must work directly with clients. And you must be a hero when it comes to bringing in big fees. While this is a constant source of irritation to the many excellent people in internal support or management roles, it is the reality of our present culture. So whatever approach we used had to include a large element of consultation with people in client-facing roles. In this way we could be sure that what we were doing was not only relevant to the business, but also respected by people throughout the firm.

KPMG has other idiosyncrasies too numerous to record here. It is worth mentioning this last one, however: we are an organisation which is very intellectual – at times too intellectual. We love ideas. In fact, we often get so carried away by new ideas that we happily rush on to debate the next one, never having paused to do anything boring like implement the last one. It is a real issue at KPMG that long-term, internal projects often run out of momentum just because people get easily distracted by new ideas. And it is ideas which win glory, not the grunt work of actually implementing them. We knew we would have to be very imaginative in our approach to ensure that interest was maintained throughout our project's long career. Moreover, with so many intellectual snobs around, anything we did needed to be pretty well thought through, and preferably quite scientific. In other words, the 'touchy feely' activities described in the last chapter such as communal foot-washing were definitely out.

KPMG's strategy for culture change Part II: The nature of the change
Having gained a fair insight into what makes KPMG 'tick', we would still have been a bit mad to run a massive programme involving thousands of people from all around the world if all we wanted to change was, say, the company car scheme. Understanding the dynamics of the organisation is only half of the equation in working out the approach. Understanding the characteristics of the specific change is the other part. Now that we know what KPMG is like, let's think about what it was we were setting out to do.

First of all, was this going to be a big change or a little change? There is an old adage, much loved by change management consultants, which says that the bigger the change, the more people should be involved in planning it. We even have a diagram to illustrate this (Figure 2.2):

Figure 2.2: *Approaches to change*

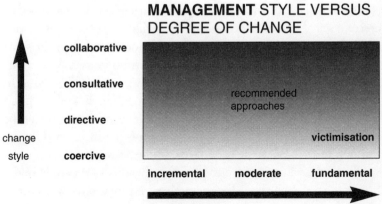

(*adapted from Dexter Dunphy and Douglas Stacy*)

For a minor change, people will generally comply even when they are given no choice about it. Involving large numbers of people in discussing small changes is an irritating waste of time. No one wants to be invited to a focus group to decide what colour the coffee cups should be (if anyone does, you might want to investigate why they have so much time on their hands). But if people are required to undertake fundamental change, for example, to their roles, location or work patterns, then unless you want all your good people to leave and your remaining staff to feel victimised, you had better consult, or even better, involve them in determining what happens to them.

Of course it is not that simple. There are other factors to take into account – such as timing, resources and the organisation dynamics which we discussed above. The prevailing management style also needs to be considered: any organisation which is used to operating in a highly directive style may have difficulty in establishing credibility for a highly participative approach and vice versa.

However, to be simplistic for a minute, at KPMG we reckoned that changing the culture of our global firm ranked as 'big' rather than 'little' (or should I say, 'fundamental' rather than 'incremental'?). Whatever happened, we knew that we had to do more than just consult; we had to get people actively involved.

Having looked at the scale of the change, we then had to think about the essence of what we were trying to achieve. Our aim was to create a set of values which would help align KPMG firms worldwide. As the timeless guiding principles for our behaviour, decisions and actions, our values needed to be relevant to every aspect of our business. Above all, they had to be shared by everyone in KPMG. In other words, we were creating a set of values which would extend well beyond the current generation of leaders and which would be owned by the whole firm, not just a few people in it. In thinking through the process to be used, a few things were clear.

First, the values needed to be uniquely KPMG's: people in the firm had to define them for themselves. No one outside the firm would be able to tell us what was good for us. Our values are intrinsic to KPMG, so we had to work them out for ourselves. Nor could we borrow values from elsewhere. Occasionally we heard comments like 'IBM's values look good – why don't we just use those?'. The answer: because we are not IBM. Our values had to capture what was *authentically believed within KPMG*, not what is good for other companies or what was calculated to be provident. It wasn't as if we were flicking through a catalogue of 'One Hundred Favourite Corporate Values Statements'.

The values needed to be shared, so a large number of KPMG people from all over the world had to be involved. It wouldn't have worked if only one person from inside the firm had developed the values. So there was no point in locking our International Chairman in a dark room and not letting him out until he had thought up a values statement that everyone would believe in. He's smart, but he's not a mass mind reader. If we wanted everyone around the world to own the values, we had to ask a lot of people around the world what they should be.

The values needed to be relevant to everyone, so the people who contributed to the process needed to come predominantly from the mainstream activities of our business. It would have been a mistake to set up a special culture change team which was separate from the rest of the organisation. If we wanted to create something which was relevant to people in the business, we had to ask people in the business to work on it.

The values had to become part of the living, breathing organism that is KPMG, so we had to make sure that our culture change process was not perceived as an invading 'foreign body'. Culture permeates every aspect of an organisation, and it follows that culture change should do the same. We did not want it to be a case of 'we need a break from the business agenda, so let's do some culture change'. The culture change process had to be integrated as far as possible with the daily workings of the organisation.

Lastly, we had to dispel the myth that culture change is lacking in any practical form of activity. It is a real, tangible process which leads to real, tangible benefits. One client once told me that their culture change team had acquired the nickname 'the fluffy slipper brigade', and this was the last thing we wanted to happen to us. Culture change is just like any other business initiative – there is a wealth of practical actions which can be undertaken to achieve it.

And now . . . KPMG's strategy for culture change
By this stage we had given consideration both to the dynamics of
KPMG and the nature of the change we were aiming to bring
about. Bringing the two together, we arrived at a strategy for
change, the key elements are:

1.   The approach was appropriately top-down
Although staff at all levels were consulted widely in the initial stages
when we were diagnosing KPMG's existing culture, and later
became involved in implementation, our focus was primarily on
KPMG's partners when it came to determining the desired values
and committing to behaviour change. We were occasionally
challenged on this by our more ardent democrats, but we felt that
our approach was nevertheless appropriate – not just because of the
partnership issues described above, but also because the definition
and implementation of values is a leadership issue. Leadership in
KPMG is the responsibility of the partners. That's why they get
paid more than everyone else. Not only that, but partners are role
models, so when it came to behaviour change, they were the ones
who would have to change first.

*2.   Thousands of people from all over the world, who came from the
mainstream of our business, needed to be involved*
As we are a global organisation, it was clear that we would have to
involve KPMG people from all over the world. To keep the values
relevant and realistic, these people needed, as far as possible, to
come from the mainstream of our business. We targeted the people
who were 'out there' doing client work and running our businesses
around the world as key contributors. We did not use consultants,
whether external or internal, in defining the content of our values
statement.

*3.   The culture change became part of our existing organisational
programme*
We did not want the culture change effort to be regarded as a
disembodied 'initiative'. As far as possible, we needed to integrate
it with our existing activities. Our solution was to utilise scheduled,

international events as far as possible. We incorporated working sessions into board meetings, conferences and training programmes, and used the time between events for further reflection and research. The advantages of this were many. First of all, it sent a clear message that the values were to be part of everyday work. Secondly, such events attracted the very people we were targeting – people from all over the world who were close to the business. Thirdly, participants were pleased, particularly at conferences, to be involved in the real-time development of our vision and strategy, so we achieved great motivation and buy-in from the very start. Of course there were also disadvantages to this approach: we had no choice about the timing of events, so sometimes the periods between them were characterised by either frenetic activity or frustrated waiting. In addition, we had to be sensitive in negotiating our involvement. We did not want to hijack events or undermine their original purpose (such pushy behaviour would hardly have been appropriate from someone promoting culture change), but we did need to create enough space to do meaningful work. On the whole, however, the advantages of this approach far outweighed the disadvantages.

> My change strategy for KPMG was to signal the new values in the change process itself. In the past, KPMG initiatives were typically run by large, exclusive working parties – which goes against our new attitude of inclusiveness. I broke from this tradition in the values initiative by assigning responsibility to just one individual – Jan Thornbury – who was not even a partner in the firm. Because no one individual could achieve – or even lead – a total culture change on this scale, I knew her efforts would have to be inclusive and integrated with existing management processes.

4. Creative approaches were used to sustain momentum
Given the fact that culture change is a lengthy business and that the collective attention span in KPMG is short when it comes to internal projects, we knew that we would have to work hard to keep the process alive. We did this by including every now and again

creative or unconventional interventions which would capture people's imagination. At the beginning, we had not a clue what form these would take, but when the time came, the right solution usually presented itself. Sometimes it was as simple as a new workshop approach at a board meeting or an interactive session at a conference, while at other times we were much more adventurous: staging soap operas, playing games or drawing pictures. The aim was always to keep the process fresh.

These four, high-level principles guided us throughout our whole process, but when we came to implementation of our desired culture, we had a few additional issues to take into account. These were largely practical considerations, but we had to adapt our strategy all the same. This is a lesson in itself: you may have a carefully developed change strategy which is working perfectly well, but it may not suffice for every phase of your process.

We had reached the stage where we had a definition of the culture we wanted to implement, and we now had to roll this out worldwide. KPMG has practices in 160 countries (plus or minus two or three, world geography being rather prone to change as well as KPMG!). Some practices had already carried out sophisticated culture change initiatives while others had done nothing. Some had a need to address a particular value while others differed. Some had suitably skilled people to run the local implementation effort while others had not. The approach to implementation of the culture change had to be flexible enough to deal with all this, as well as the inevitable differences in national culture.

Because of the great need for flexibility we could not prescribe one particular approach for everyone. We also knew that people in KPMG don't like being told what to do and that it was important to keep the responsibility and ownership of the culture change at a local level. Our approach to implementation was therefore facilitative rather than prescriptive. Prior to the implementation phase we had had one process which included everyone. Now it looked like that was no longer practical, so instead of designing one implementation programme for everyone, we enabled people to develop their own processes. We provided people with practical advice and a range of tools and techniques from which they could put together the culture change programme which best suited their own, local KPMG practices. People were therefore able to focus on the things they needed to do most and, in their own way, move towards our common goal.

Short-term strategies and long-term dreams
Our dream is that in the longer term there will be no need for a 'culture change' initiative at KPMG, because our new values will be integral to everything we do. In the short-term however, a distinct culture change programme is needed to raise awareness of the importance of our new values. As we make the transition to our ideal culture, we will ensure that our new values become as much part of daily life at KPMG as possible. In the short- to medium-term, we will aim to integrate our culture change activities even more fully with our existing organisational programme.

Culture change without hocus-pocus
At KPMG we tried to take the mystique out of culture change. We made sure that throughout the process, our change effort was characterised by practical actions and tangible results. The approach we took was very straightforward and could be applied in any organisation.

At the highest level, the method is very simple. Of course, like most things that look simple on the surface, 'the devil is in the detail', but we will go into that in subsequent chapters. For now, let's look at the very basics of what is needed. (By the way, if you prefer a little mystique, the explanation is given in Management Consulting Speak on the right in addition to the Plain English version on the left.)

I have found that in many organisations, people are tempted to neglect the first step of truly understanding their present culture. They argue that as they wish to create a new culture, there is no point in dwelling on what exists now. I wonder at this, because I don't believe the same people would get into their cars on a Sunday afternoon and set out for a remote destination without first being sure of where they were starting from. Understanding the existing culture is essential. In *any* change process, you need to know where

<table>
<tr><td colspan="3">A process for culture change:</td></tr>
</table>

	Plain English	*Management Consulting Speak*
Step 1	Work out where you are now	Diagnose the present culture
Step 2	Decide where you want to go	Define the desired culture
Step 3	Do what you need to do to get there	Implement the organisational and behavioural changes necessary to bring the desired culture into being

you are starting from so that you can prioritise actions to get where you want to go. For example, suppose you wanted to become fluent in a foreign language. You would first need to establish your current level of proficiency so that you knew whether to join a beginners', intermediate or advanced language class. The same principles apply to culture change.

Another good reason for being thorough at this first stage is that when your culture change process commences, you will be operating *in* the present culture. Any changes you make will be resisted or supported by it. To be able to anticipate difficulties, to manage resistance effectively, and to design interventions which work, you will need to understand the present culture, warts-and-all. If you want to change the culture you are in, you will need to push back some boundaries. But before you try that, it's handy if you know where those boundaries *are*.

A third reason for making sure that you have an accurate picture of the present culture is that you are unlikely to want to change it too drastically or all at once. The present culture is a fundamental part of your company's identity. It will have benefits and strengths which it would be disastrous to lose. If you think your whole corporate culture stinks and needs to be turned into something completely different then maybe you should just go and join another company. Of course anyone leading a culture change effort needs to be dissatisfied with the present state of affairs. Otherwise, what would be the motivation to change? But when you do take an in-depth look at your present culture you might be surprised to find that there are a lot of features you wish to preserve and strengthen. Only a thorough analysis of the present culture will bring these to light.

When researching the existing culture you need to seek a wide range of opinion. This is because people at different levels in the organisation will have different perceptions – and experiences – of the culture. To gain a balanced picture you need to ask around. At subsequent stages of the process it may be appropriate, as it was at KPMG, to adopt a more top-down approach, but at this stage you cannot afford to do that.

When it comes to the second stage of the culture change process, the desired culture may be defined in such vague terms that you will have no idea about what to implement. The mistake that is commonly made is to define the desired culture in terms which are too abstract. As a result, it is hard to determine what actions might be taken or what the tangible outcomes of the culture change might be. For example, throughout my career as a consultant to client organisations, the subject of trust has often come up. In describing their desired culture, people say things like 'We need to build a culture of trust' or 'We need to trust each other more'. So what actions can you take on this? Do you get them to look into each other's eyes and say 'I trust you'? That won't help, except to produce a temporary feeling of confidence.

The secret is to paint a picture of the desired culture in *graphic detail*. It is not sufficient just to draw up a new values statement. That alone is not a rich enough image of the desired culture. People have to understand exactly what that values statement means in real life. So in addition to the values, they will need to be clear on what the other layers of culture will look like. In particular, they will need to identify what behaviours they will see in the new culture to support the new values – and name the behaviours which they no longer wish to see. So if we go back to the example above, people would need to be more specific about what 'trust' looks like. What *exactly* do they need to *do* – and stop doing – to *show* that they trust one another? To complete the picture of the desired culture, specific descriptions of 'do' and 'don't' behaviours are essential.

To further enhance the description of the desired culture, it is worth considering what the tangible outcomes of the culture change might be. 'How will you know when you have got there?' is a question often posed by management consultants to clients undertaking major change. It is an irritating question, but only because it forces you to think. It prompts you to imagine you are already in the desired, future state – what do you see? What is different from now? Answering such questions helps you recognise what the benefits will be. It also helps you define how you will measure progress when the change is underway. Perhaps most importantly, it helps you 'feel' what the new culture will be like. This is all part of the vision which you will need to motivate you throughout the change process.

At the third stage – implementation – basic rules apply like in any other change programme. The design phase is over and now you actually have to start *doing stuff*. This is where most culture change efforts fail, because people rack their brains but can't think of any practical actions to undertake. Often this is because not enough effort was put into defining the desired culture in the first place. If you are not specific about the desired culture, action plans will be equally woolly. For example, 'We will be nice to each other' is hardly an action which you could include in a project plan, though you would be surprised by how often people propose things like this as solutions. Culture change is all about making organisational and behaviour changes in a pragmatic and practical way. You will need to define your actions clearly and impose some time-frames. In fact, you should be able to write down what you are doing in a project plan.

Culture is slow to change, so implementation will be the longest phase. It is vital to maintain momentum. It is often the case that in the initial stages of implementation, a great deal of effort is being expended for what looks like not much in return. This can lead to frustration. As time progresses, people tend to stop being frustrated and just get bored. Programme managers often make the mistake of pouring all their creativity into the initial phases of the culture change process. Then, when it comes to implementation, they resort to traditional methods used on plodding, long-term projects. In a way, it is even more important to be creative in the implementation phase than it is in the first two stages of the process. The first two phases of the process are lively and interesting enough in themselves. With implementation, you have to work at it.

Another vital ingredient which tends to diminish during implementation is sponsorship from the leadership team. Leaders of organisations have plenty of things to worry about without the extra burden of their commitment to long-term projects. In addition, they will find during the implementation phase that they themselves are no longer expected just to *talk* about culture change – they actually have to *do* it. And that might mean some serious work on their own behaviour. The leadership's commitment is essential throughout the process, but implementation is the phase where you will probably have to invest the most effort in maintaining it.

There is one more, fundamental point which you must not forget. You need to bear it in mind throughout all stages of process – and before you even start. It's the answer to the following, simple question about culture change:

'Why bother?'

If energy and enthusiasm for the culture change process are starting to flag, or if your sponsors on the leadership team are backsliding, you will need to remind people of the compelling reasons why the organisation set out on this route in the first place. What is the business case for changing your culture?

It is amazing how often the business case is overlooked in culture change, and this can be devastating when it comes to maintaining momentum and sponsorship. Most organisations would never dream of undertaking any other type of initiative without a sound economic reason. Can you imagine justifying investment in a new IT system by saying that everybody will probably feel good when the system's in? Yet culture change initiatives are frequently justified on such shaky grounds. In good times, leaders of organisations might like to be magnanimous, and making people happy might be enough reason to invest in a culture change programme. However, as soon as pressure is on (and where isn't the pressure on in business these days?), that culture change initiative will likely be abandoned in favour of another project which more obviously delivers tangible business benefits.

> When I first decided that culture change at KPMG was necessary to our future success, what made me pause was the enormity of the challenge. There was such a gigantic chasm between where the organisation was culturally, and where it needed to be. 'Could we actually bridge that gulf?' I wondered. It was clear, however, that we had no choice – the business case was overwhelming. We had to try, whatever the outcome.

Before embarking on a process of culture change, you therefore need to assemble some pretty compelling arguments for what you are about to undertake. What threats in the business environment do you think you will avoid through successful culture change? How will changing help you to take advantage of opportunities? What competitive benefits will a new culture bring? There also needs to be a strong sense of urgency: bear in mind that distant threats and opportunities are not nearly as motivating as those which are just around the corner.

At KPMG, we took a long look at what our clients were expecting, what our competitors were doing, and the increasingly difficult struggle which all professional service organisations have in attracting and retaining talented people. We looked at our statistics. We pondered on our strengths and weaknesses. We investigated opportunities and threats. We saw an urgent need to globalise. We saw that a new culture would give us a competitive advantage. All in all, it was not difficult to demonstrate the benefits a culture change would bring. And we made links with how culture change would help us to achieve our strategic goals and improve our bottom-line performance. Our business case was 100% sound, and even then, it was sometimes a struggle to maintain momentum.

If you cannot justify your culture change effort with a rock-solid business case, then you really should ask yourself why you are bothering. Culture change is one of the most difficult initiatives which an organisation can undertake – it is complex and slow. It cannot be managed in a neat, sequential way like many other big projects. It involves individuals changing their behaviour, which is perhaps the most demanding thing you will ever ask them to do. Given all this, even the most ardent of do-gooders might recognise that culture change should not be undertaken without good reason. Think about your business case. What benefits will culture change bring? What threats might a change in culture help your organisation to avoid? How will a change in culture give your business a competitive advantage? If you are convinced by your answers to these questions then you will have the momentum to keep you progressing along the path to a better culture.

Culture Δ is not a project...
it is a process.

Chapter 3

THE PRINCIPLES IN ACTION

In the last chapter, we looked in detail at the theory behind culture and culture change. We also talked about how important it is to consider the context within which you are operating before you embark on culture change (or any major change programme). Now it is time to put these principles into action, and to talk about what we did at KPMG and what actually happened on a day-to-day basis.

The first thing to understand is that this was not a 'project'. Projects have clearly defined beginnings, middles and ends. This didn't, and it is unlikely that any other culture change you encounter will fit neatly into that format. Culture change is better described as a *process*, because there isn't a clear start or finish point. In our case, it is hard to pin down exactly when the process began, because all sorts of activities and attitudes built up to it. It is also difficult to categorise all that has been done into neat phases, because activities overlapped, unexpected ideas and opportunities were utilised along the way and at times we had to 'go with the flow'. Finally, while you can tell when a project has ended, with a process, you can never be sure. At KPMG although we asked people to describe 'how we will know when we have got there', I suspect that when we do 'get there', there will still be more to do. The good thing about managing a process is that you can get away with not doing a project plan. In fact, you need to get someone to manage it who is responsive to the changing organisation and who actively doesn't want to impose rigid start- and end-dates or milestone charts. Colin was a boss who understood this perfectly. It's the first time in my life someone has regarded my allergy to project planning as a good thing.

In managing a process, as opposed to a project, it is hard to explain to people in advance exactly what you will be doing and when. You can only describe this in retrospect. In other words, it is like going on a journey, but not one where you have planned your route or booked your accommodation in advance. It is like setting off on a long trip with only a backpack and a guidebook, rather than going on the organised tour. You have a clear vision of what it is you want to do, but you can't say before you go that you will be in a certain place on a certain day. With the detail, you make it up as you go along. Diaries are good ways of describing journeys, and they make interesting reading even if the journey has not yet finished, so I will describe the process we followed in a similar way.

Diary of the process

Before the beginning

The beginning is impossible to pin down, but let's choose it arbitrarily as the first event which we used to kick off the values process for KPMG International. This took place in May 1997, and was the meeting of KPMG's International Council where Colin launched the 'virtual firm' strategy. Specifically, the Council would be asked to work on the elements of that strategy which concerned values and core services. But let's start here before the beginning, and trace some of the roots of the values work.

KPMG UK, 1995–96

Colin's interest in culture change had started a long time before 1997. I became aware of it in autumn 1995, when he was running KPMG's UK practice and I was working in the firm as a management consultant. As part of a wider programme looking at leadership issues, I was asked to do some research into the culture of KPMG in the UK. KPMG's British practice was a sizeable organisation with about 10,000 people. We surveyed the whole UK firm using a proprietary questionnaire which measured the extent to which twelve behavioural styles were present in the organisation. The survey we used is a well-validated tool in which behaviours are classified into three basic categories: constructive, aggressive-defensive and passive-defensive. It is oversimplifying somewhat to say that constructive behaviours are deemed good and all defensive behaviours are regarded as bad, but that is broadly how the results are to be interpreted.

No one was surprised when KPMG UK's survey resulted in a profile of appalling behaviour to be proud of. There was a lot of macho, aggressive-defensive behaviour, and there was also a fair measure of passive-defensiveness thrown in so that no one would feel left out. The only behaviours that were underrepresented were the constructive variety (no one in KPMG likes a goody-goody). The picture was broadly uniform all over the country and across disciplines, though a few departments were anxious to point out that 'our profile is two percentiles better than the average . . .' (competitiveness was a marked trait!). An analysis of the results by grade revealed that the perception of the culture got progressively worse with increasing levels of seniority. Except when you reached the level of the partnership, that is. The partners' perception of the culture, while far from rosy, was markedly more positive than that of the staff at the level immediately below them. Well, let's not speculate here on why that was the case, but note again how important it is to gather views from a representative cross-section of employees when assessing the current culture.

As I said earlier, surveys can only give a limited picture of an organisation's culture, and it is a crude picture. However, this survey had the advantage of providing comparisons with world-class organisations and their profiles looked somewhat different from ours. The suppliers also had data which linked constructive behaviour profiles with strong financial performance. On seeing the link between constructive behaviours and organisational performance, the partnership of the UK firm, always keen to make more money, became interested. They started to realise that there may be some material benefit to all this touchy feely stuff after all. So while we only had a very tenuous picture of a small part of our culture, interest and awareness had been kindled and, unknown to any of us at the time, we had set foot on the road to major culture change.

After the survey, we spent some time working with individuals, pretty much exclusively at the level of the most senior partners, to help them reflect on and change their behaviour to become better role models. This did do some good, but it was a little bit like chipping away at an iceberg with a teaspoon. It certainly wasn't enough to bring about a sustainable culture change. But we did not know what to do at that point, for all the reasons I mentioned in the last chapter. We did not *really* know where we were starting from, because the culture survey had provided us with only one piece of a very complex jigsaw. And we certainly had not formulated clearly where we wanted to go. We were fumbling around in the dark and it soon became clear that it was time to look at our culture, and the culture we wanted, in much more depth.

In mid-1996, Colin gave me a full-time job in his advisory team and a few months later he called me into his office and gave me one of his customary, highly detailed briefs. 'I want to know what the values are out there,' he said. 'Go and find out what people think.'

Around this time, values statements in the UK firm were popping up like mushrooms in a wet field. Every office, business unit, interest group or even, it seemed, bunch of four or five casual acquaintances seemed to have thought up its own code of values. I made a few inquiries and gathered a motley mix of about ten different values statements. These were just the values statements which I found out about in what was, even by my standards, a relatively idle morning's work. If I had made a more serious effort goodness knows how many I would have uncovered. Some of these statements had been carefully researched, considered and well articulated. Some had been scribbled on the back of an envelope. Some had been poached from a competitor. Some had been brain-dumped in over-zealous team-bonding exercises. Some were contradictory. Some were great. Some were awful. None of them were real.

None of them were real because they were all *espoused* values, wish-lists or aspirations. In other words, they didn't reflect the true culture, so I still could not answer Colin's question. Answering Colin's question I guessed would be easy enough with the right kind of research. But in the meantime, we had unearthed another problem. With a multitude of different values statements, we had a classic example of KPMG's wheel-reinvention habit at its worst. Because however much or however little effort had been put into the development of those many creeds, I knew that their owners were going to be very attached to them. Faced with such a glaring lack of alignment, I tried to see the positive side. It was absolutely clear that if busy people in KPMG were making time to develop values statements, they must have felt a very strong need for change, they must have already recognised that it was time KPMG did something to improve its culture. Who could blame them for doing it themselves? They didn't want to hang around and at that point, no one had addressed the subject firm-wide.

To come back to Colin's question, which was 'What are the values out there?', we conducted some in-depth research into the current culture. We had reached a point where survey question-naires no longer sufficed, so the approach we adopted from then on was purely qualitative. In other words, we talked to a lot of people. In the previous chapter, we discussed how an analysis of behaviour is the first step in understanding the values of an organisation, and this is the route we took in the research.

We wanted to be sure to capture representative views from all across the organisation, so we ran an extensive series of focus groups and interviews. Participants came from all levels, functions and locations within the UK firm. Sometimes the focus group participants were mixed with regard to function and grade, and sometimes they were completely homogeneous. Interviewees ranged widely, from senior partners to secretaries.

Our method was to first identify the behaviour patterns in the firm and then to use these as a basis for working back to the values which underpin these behaviours.

To identify the behaviour patterns, we developed a fun but very effective method which was christened 'The Hustler's Guide to getting on in KPMG' by a focus group participant. In focus groups and interviews, we asked people to imagine that their best friend had joined KPMG and wanted to do well. We asked what would be the off-the-record, absolutely honest advice which they would give that person? Specifically:

- 'What are the things you *must* do?'
- 'What are the things you *can get away with not* doing?'
- 'What are the things you *absolutely must never* do?'

This produced results which were searing in their honesty – good and bad traits in KPMG were brought to light time after time. I was amazed at the similarity in views between groups and individuals. Irrespective of seniority, location or function, people had no trouble describing graphically 'the way we do things around here – how it *really* is'. And, since a few witty people always seemed to emerge, we also had a lot of fun. Having fun was important – I certainly did not want to trivialise the process, but was also well aware that without some sort of novelty in the approach, each focus group had the potential to develop into a version of the aforementioned Monumental Bitching Session. It is always a fine balance to preserve the integrity of the work without making things dull or overly serious. In these sessions, we took care to explain the process and to explain the theory and motivation behind what we were doing. In that way, people were willing and more able to contribute usefully to the content of the discussion. And of course, we made the process safe by never attributing any of the comments people made.

After identifying the behaviour patterns, we delved into the values using an iterative questioning technique. So you were asleep the last time I explained what this is? Well, in other words, we asked *why* the Hustler's Guide really was the acceptable way to behave in KPMG. What were the values underpinning these behaviours? We kept asking *why* until we felt we had arrived at the underlying value. This was harder to do, and required a lot of reflecting back on the behaviours which had been identified. We always sought to begin by looking at a particular behaviour and asking 'Why do we behave like this?' rather than asking 'What are the values?' because we felt that in this way people would be more objective and base anything they said about the values on facts and observations. If anyone did make a direct statement about the values we always checked back to see if there were any behaviours which provided evidence to support their views.

When we felt we had a list of current values, we started to ask which were core. We did this by asking which were the fundamentally important values which people in the firm would never, ever give up. To emphasise the point, we asked people to imagine a strange world where maintaining a certain value had a negative impact on our business. Would we stick to the value anyway and go into a different business where it was still important or would we rather abandon it for the sake of expediency? It was easy to identify some of the core values in this way, but others were debated furiously. This was not surprising, as values are pretty emotive. Eventually we arrived at the few values and beliefs which people felt were at the core of KPMG's existing culture.

After a while, all the focus groups and interviewees seemed to be saying the same thing, so we stopped, as we believed that this was validation that we had enough representation and that we had gathered all the information we were going to get. I later found out that the focus group population we had used matched almost exactly what is recommended in textbooks. So it really does work. Statistical sampling theory, I mean.

I wrote a report for the UK Board giving an in-depth description of KPMG's present culture. The Board liked it, especially the Hustler's Guide, which I slipped in as an appendix although I did at the time wonder whether it would cost me my career (you see, the Hustler's Guide itself advised strongly against being impertinent). The positive reaction of senior management resulted I think because humour, at least in the UK, often softens the blow of absolute honesty. The Hustler's Guide was descriptive but not accusing, so they were able to read it, laugh, and then acknowledge that this is exactly how it is. (It also contained the word 'bullshit' which I think made a few of the Board members feel thrilled at how daring and progressive we were becoming.)

The next step was to decide what the present culture of KPMG UK needed to change. We began working with the UK Board to develop a picture of our desired culture, and we began to plan a comprehensive change programme. However, we had barely begun when everything altered because Colin was appointed as KPMG's

International Chairman. The 'virtual firm' strategy was born, and I suddenly had to extend my remit to KPMG globally.

KPMG International – before May 1997
While the UK practice had been working on its culture, other KPMG national practices had not been idle. Many of them had come to the same conclusion that something needed to be done about the firm's culture and they were having plenty of ideas. Already several initiatives were in place at a local level.

Our American practice had developed a set of values and tied these in with their vision and strategy. Their communication of these values and the commitment of their leadership team were admirable. They had integrated their values into many HR processes, particularly in assessment and reward, where they said that in addition to conventional performance indicators such as financial targets, people would also be assessed on whether or not they behaved according to the values. They had – and this is unusual in KPMG – made a pledge of 'zero tolerance', that is, they promised to get tough on people who undermined their values.

Our Dutch practice had been involved in an ongoing programme of culture change for years. They had involved large numbers of people from within their practice in a strategy and organisation development process called 'Vision 2000'. (Now that we are actually *in* the third millennium, 'Vision 2000' sounds a little passé, but you have to bear in mind that this work was done in the mid-1990s, and was then ahead of its time.)

KPMG New Zealand had also done extensive work on values. They linked values with brand image, making the very valid connection that what we look like to the outside world should reflect what we are like on the inside.

The senior team of our Canadian practice had developed a new vision and strategy document which included a set of values, as had our French practice.

And so on and so on.

Thankfully, not all of KPMG's 160 practices worldwide had done their own thing to address the matter of culture. Many had done nothing at all! But nonetheless, we had a plethora of unaligned values statements out there. Values initiatives were mushrooming again, but this time the field was much, much bigger. I consoled myself with the fact that at least there was an interest and a recognised need among some of our national practices for a clear set of values. I also thought that although it was bigger, it was essentially the same problem that we had had in the UK, so if we could resolve it once we would be able to fix it again. But in an organisation which still operated in federal mode, with a high degree of local autonomy, would our attempt to develop a global set of values be perceived as treading on people's toes? It was clear that any process which we used to develop a set of shared values for our big, global firm would have to be sensitive to what had gone before at a local level. Not only that, but we did not want to let any good work go to waste. The first thing we did was simply to gather all the information we had into one big pot – asking everyone what had been done locally and treating it as input to the international process. I guessed that when all this input reappeared at some later stage, people would be reassured that their work had made a contribution.

Phase 1: Understanding the Present Culture

KPMG International Council Workshop, Dublin, May 1997
The event which marks the beginning of the process (in as far as any event can) is a meeting of KPMG's International Council which took place at the end of May 1997. The International Council consists of the senior partners of KPMG's top 25 practices, plus representatives from practices of strategic importance, regional representatives, international executive partners and the chairman. In other words, it is the top thirty-six of KPMG's most senior guys, whose practices, if you add them all together, bring in the greater part by a long way of the firm's total global revenue. The Council meets twice yearly. Their role is a combination of Supervisory Board, Supreme Court and that ruling body of wise elders that you get in *Star Trek* films. (The more official role description is that they are KPMG International's ultimate governing body and represent the shareholders.)

The Council meeting in May 1997 was the first to be run with Colin as International Chairman. It was at this event that he gained approval for the 'virtual firm' strategy and he also allocated a day on the agenda to develop it further. The Council was to spend time working on two elements of the strategy: values and core services. Council meetings had, in the past, been very formal, consisting mainly of plenary sessions with multiple presentations. Colin felt that this format was too boring and a hindrance to the group doing meaningful work. He wanted to change the style of the meeting altogether to include different ways of working. He invited myself and my colleagues to use a workshop approach to encourage the Council to think about values and core services in a more creative way.

> The May 1997 meeting of the KPMG International Council in Dublin was the first occasion when Council members were asked to consider the future of the firm. There were thirty-six of us there, from all over the world, focusing for several days on the single issue of our culture and aspirations. I was a bit worried whether they might resent it as an airy-fairy waste of a meeting. But their reaction was the opposite: they expressed both relief and a sense of urgency. 'At last we're doing something! It's about time.'

Because we were at the start of the culture change process for KPMG International, I chose to use the meeting to focus on diagnosing the firm's *existing* culture. I had a fair idea of what to expect. From my previous work, I already had an accurate view of what the culture was like in the UK. I also had my own memories (all pleasant) of five years working for KPMG in Germany. In addition, I had trawled through various attitude survey results and culture change initiatives from KPMG offices around the world and chatted informally to individuals from different countries. I had found that most of this research had indicated more similarities than differences in KPMG's culture around the world, but I was well aware that the evidence was patchy and I have always been a stickler for valid statistics. Anyway, I felt that our views of the existing culture needed some validation in the international context, and what better group to do that than this diverse, globally representative bunch of KPMG lifers?

In addition to the basic need of validating our findings on the existing culture, there was a second, more subtle need which was much more important: this was the first event in the values process, and the success of the process would depend on whether or not we were able to engage the firm's international leadership. So it was vital that the approach we took would be interesting and compelling enough to help the Council commit to the process.

There were two things which I felt would help engage the group: One was to make them aware of the business case for culture change and the other was to provide an innovative approach for them to work on the issues.

We addressed the business case with the whole group in a plenary session. We talked about what was facing KPMG International, focusing on globalisation and the need for alignment. We also addressed some of the issues we felt that a culture change would help resolve: our need to win more value-added work, our difficulties with staff retention, our struggle to maintain consistency around the world and so on. In addition, we looked at examples from outside KPMG and the sector in which we operate and saw that companies with strong cultures simply perform better. In other words, whether we were looking at ourselves or looking outside, it was clear that there was a significant benefit to be gained through strengthening our culture in the right way.

The second means to engage the Council was the process we used in the meeting as they worked on the values. It had to be different from the traditional style of meeting to which they were accustomed. It had to be interesting and lively but not frivolous, and they had to become actively involved in thinking, discussing and doing meaningful work. The group was too big to manage in a workshop context, so we split them into smaller groups of about seven or eight people. Each group was allocated an experienced facilitator. In other words, we had five facilitated mini-workshops running simultaneously. In these, we used a process which was practically identical to the focus group process I had designed for researching the current culture in KPMG in the UK. Curiously though, when we ran the 'Hustler's Guide' exercise about how to get on in KPMG, the behaviours which were named by the Council as 'must do' 'can get away with not doing' and 'absolutely must not do' were strikingly similar to what I had found out in my extensive focus group work in the UK. Maybe we did have a global culture after all. (A summary of the Hustler's Guide is given in Table 3.1.)

Working from the behaviours listed by each group, we identified the underlying values and then proceeded to differentiate which were core and which were not. Some were so obvious that they were no-brainers, while on other topics, views did seem to vary a little. In the end we achieved agreement on the following set of current, core values. These also agreed closely with research done elsewhere in the firm:

- Serving the client comes first
- Individualism
- Technical excellence and professional standards
- Integrity

All these values have positive qualities which we were keen to preserve. However, we also recognised inherent negative aspects which in our desired culture we would seek to minimise. More specifically:

- *Serving the client comes first* is a very worthy sentiment, and if you read the Hustler's Guide from the client perspective, you would probably feel pretty reassured that you were going to get excellent service. KPMG has always been very client-focused and wishes to remain so. However, there were some subtleties to this which needed to be changed. One group at the Council meeting summarised our approach to client relationships in the phrase 'the client is king'. This is great if you're the king but not so hot if you're a peasant at risk of getting his head chopped off. In a similar vein, another group pointed out that they had deliberately used the words 'serving the client' rather than saying 'working

Table 3.1: The Hustler's Guide to Getting on in KPMG

Frank advice from hundreds of partners and staff from around the world on how to succeed in the firm according to the old rules (1996–97)

What you MUST do	*What you CAN GET AWAY WITH NOT doing*	*What you absolutely MUST NOT do*
• Be committed to clients above all else	• All internal commitments	• Put anything before clients
• Be linked to prestigious clients	• Most administrative tasks	• Break ethical guidelines, be dishonest or unprofessional
• Align yourself with a successful partner as your sponsor	• Abiding by internal rules (e.g. 'clean desk' and travel policies)	• Divulge client confidentiality
• Play the politics	• Being on time (Hint: client work is a great excuse for this)	• Lose important clients
• Be sociable, build relationships and get on with people, both internally and externally	• Delegating properly	• Upset clients
• Collect excellent people around you	• Assisting or briefing other people	• Show disloyalty
• Take and make opportunities	• Sharing knowledge and information	• Get into litigation or generate bad publicity
• Have personal ambition which benefits the firm	• Sharing resources	• Be rude or disrespectful
• Be visible – Blow your own trumpet	• Saying what you're really feeling	• Ask about pay
• Have integrity and honesty	• Entering into discussions on profitability	• Dress scruffily or unconventionally
• Get the numbers	• Coaching and	• Have a 9 to 5 attitude
		• Have a track record of failures
		• Be so aggressive that you're hated
		• Wait for solutions
		• Put in less than

behind your name (Bring in high fees, and lots of client relationships)

- Put the firm first – 'Your first wife is KPMG'
- Be seen to work long hours (Hint: buy two jackets – one to wear and one to drape over the back of your chair when you go home)
- Exhibit professional excellence and technical competence
- Appear to know what you are doing
- Have common sense
- Deliver on time and to budget
- Be able to bullshit
- Look for short-term wins
- Rock the boat a little, but not too much
- It's often luck – be in the right place at the right time

developing others

- Your own training, development or counselling
- Making decisions (Hint: form a committee instead!)
- Long-term thinking
- Taking special risks
- Helping to sell services outside your own area of expertise
- Taking responsibility for your own mistakes and disasters
- Justifying actions with business cases
- Thinking globally
- Everything not related to the bottom line

100% of effort

- Upset key decision-makers
- Neglect to manage risk properly
- Admit your limitations
- Publicise your mistakes
- Any internal projects

with clients', because sometimes people at KPMG can be *too* accommodating, and do anything the client says, often at the expense of staff. The Council wanted to keep our strong client focus but agreed that the nature of the client relationship needed to become more robust, more value-adding and to assume more of a partnership character.

- *Individualism* was thought to manifest itself in a number of ways. The enormous positive advantage is that KPMG people are definitely not a bunch of 'clones'. People are allowed to be themselves. Because the firm values individualism, this promotes autonomy and freedom which in turn encourages creativity and entrepreneurship. However, individualism has an unpleasant side too. There is a 'what's in it for me?' attitude which encourages people to act like lone heroes, and the competitive nature of individualism can lead to ineffective teamworking and poor sharing of knowledge and resources.

- *Technical excellence and professional standards* – KPMG is proud of its reputation for technical excellence. In addition to an almost religious adhesion to standards dictated by, say, accounting bodies there is also a passion for quality in the more general sense. However, there is an extent to which these characteristics are perceived in the marketplace as 'givens'. In other words, something we need just to be in the market. We could not imagine too many clients rubbing their hands together with glee and saying 'Oh goody – I'm getting such good compliance with professional standards when I hire KPMG'. They expect that anyway, and when did anything ever excite you when you expected it? While there was no question of abandoning these values, the Council felt that our notion of what constitutes 'quality' needed to be broadened. We needed to think more about what would be of value to the client, and this goes beyond the technically faultless solution. In other words, we might be proud of producing a lengthy, immaculate report, but if the client is looking for some creative ideas or quick fixes, this may not be what is regarded as 'quality'.

- *Integrity* – In the group which I was facilitating, everyone claimed straight away that integrity in client relationships was a core value. I nevertheless decided to test this with a question about whether, in a strange world where integrity no longer mattered, we would nevertheless keep it as a value.

  'But integrity will always matter!' they cried in indignation.

  'Yes, but just *imagine* a strange world where it didn't matter so much. Would you still stick to that value?'

  'But there is no such world!'

  'But *suppose* there was, would you still . . .'

  'But it will never be like that! Without integrity we are dead!'

  So much for out-of-the-box questioning techniques. I guessed by then it was time for me to give up hypothesising. We had clearly found something which is so dear to KPMG that we would never give it up, irrespective of the circumstances.

While we had secured broad agreement on what was valued by KPMG, we thought it was worth reflecting on what did *not* appear to be part of the current values system. What was missing from our present culture, which really ought to have been there? Three key issues emerged:

- Many of the Council members, not to mention the people questioned in the background research, felt that KPMG did not value its people enough. When asked to mark KPMG's treatment of staff on a continuum between 'we treat people as an expendable resource' and 'we respect, nurture and support our people', most Council members said we were about halfway between the two extremes (staff in the UK said this too, by the way, but added that they thought KPMG, although it could do better, was nevertheless ahead of our competitors on this issue). So while the picture wasn't completely bleak, there was substantial room for improvement.

- Openness and trust *within* the firm were deemed to be lacking, so while KPMG people were fanatical about maintaining their integrity with clients, in the maelstrom of office politics this was not always evident in dealings with *each other*. (I guess it's where the nasty side of individualism comes into play.)
- KPMG seemed to really struggle when it came to sharing knowledge internally. This was partly a manifestation of individualism, as knowledge is a source of power, but it was perhaps also to do with becoming distracted before learning could be captured or shared, or simply not valuing enough the knowledge we had.

We had reached a fair conclusion on the current values, even though the discussions had not been easy (and there was still debate about claims that one particular practice really did treat its people extraordinarily well in comparison to all the others). However, as discussions on values go, we could declare victory. We had pretty much validated our previous diagnoses of KPMG's existing culture and we had engaged the Council in a lively discussion which was a first step in gaining their longer-term buy-in. All in all, it would have been a breeze, had the discussions not taken another turn, as is often the case when you start taking the lid off things.

When the five facilitators got together after the small group discussions to pool their findings, we found we had all had similar experiences. We had found that there was broad agreement on topics relating to the firm's values. But every group, in one form or another, had also discussed the firm's *purpose*. There had been at times heated debates from which no clear picture of the firm's *raison d'être* emerged.

Let's pause for a minute to say what we mean by 'core purpose'. We use Collins and Porras's definition (*Built to Last*, 3rd edition, Random House Business Books, 2000), in which core purpose is defined as one of the components of a company's enduring core ideology:

$$Core\ Ideology = Core\ Values + Core\ Purpose$$

where

> Core values are the organisation's essential and enduring tenets
> – a small set of general guiding principles, not to be confused
> with specific cultural or operating practices; not to be
> compromised for financial gain or short-term expediency
>
> Core purpose is the organisation's fundamental reason for
> existing beyond just making money – a perpetual guiding star on
> the horizon, not to be confused with specific goals or business
> strategies

Defined in simple terms, we thought of core purpose as our reason for being and the core values as the guiding principles for how we conduct our business, how we interact and the decisions we make. Both these are enduring, timeless even, and both are fundamental to the company's vision.

Why had we got into discussions about core purpose when we had set out to discuss values? Because it is impossible to address one of these without the other. Many diversions from the values discussion led us to this fundamental question. For example, we discussed the importance of money. Some Council members argued that KPMG exists solely to make money, and that this was the only thing which was important to our people. Others were scandalised by this attitude, saying learning and the feeling of doing something worthwhile was our main motivator. (We did point out that if money was the only important thing, why didn't we go off and do something really profitable like become drugs barons, and even the most hardened materialists conceded that maybe there was a little more to it than that.)

Taking money aside, as something which follows as a natural consequence of running a successful business, why were we here? If KPMG had shut down operations that night at midnight, what would the world be missing out on the next day? Some recalled our then mission statement and said we were here to provide advisory services. Others groaned at this. Was our reason for existence to do audits? To run business process improvement projects? Hardly.

That might be part of what we *do* on a day-to-day basis, but somewhat sad as a reason for existence.

The issue of identity was also unclear. In several groups it was hotly debated whether we should model ourselves on a particular competitor, famous not only for its aggression, strict rules and clone-like staff but also for its competitiveness, high fee income and technical excellence. Some Council members felt we should emulate them, while others felt that this was the absolute antithesis of how we should act. Either way, there was disagreement about what we should fundamentally *be*.

As the facilitators pieced together the input from the five different groups, it became clear that there needed to be some more fundamental thinking about our core purpose as well as our values.

Later that day, we reported back to the Council in a plenary session. On the whole, it had been an agreeable day, and the Council were on good form when we got up to present our findings. A colleague and I began the presentation by summarising what we had found out about values and behaviours across KPMG. There was a lot of nodding and smiling. The Council are a nice bunch of people, and we started to relax in response to their amiable reception as the presentation continued. When the time came to raise the subject of purpose, I blithely continued by saying that in the course of the discussions, another related issue had arisen and in fact it seemed that there was no shared sense of purpose for the global firm. This statement was greeted by a sudden, stunned silence in which I thought I had mistakenly wandered on to the wrong film set. Any worries I had had about being the light entertainment at the meeting rapidly disappeared. We responded with a stunned silence of our own – why the surprise? Weren't we just saying something that everyone knew already? Not only that, but we were only reflecting back what they had said themselves a few hours before. I still haven't fully worked out why they seemed so shocked – maybe they were saying to themselves 'We said that?', or maybe they were thinking 'Where did Colin find that impertinent young woman?'. My own theory is that the Council members did know *intuitively* what the firm's purpose was, and so they were all the more shocked to find that they had difficulty in articulating it. And it was clear that if they could not articulate it precisely in a Council meeting, what hope was there for the people in the rest of the firm?

Whatever the reason, the result was that some serious work was put into articulating our core purpose after that. The Council decided that by the next meeting of our International Board (this group of twelve is a sub-group of the International Council and functions as a management board), a new purpose statement would be finalised.

The International Board revises the Mission Statement, Berlin, July 1997
The statement of purpose had to be simple, clear and profound all at once. It had to encapsulate precisely why KPMG exists. It had to be something that everyone in the firm, irrespective of their role, would understand. It also had to be something which would make our people proud to be part of KPMG.

After some deep thought and consultation on Colin's part, he developed the purpose statement which the Board approved a few months later. KPMG's core purpose is:

> 'To turn knowledge into value for the benefit of its clients, its people and its communities'

This meant modifying the firm's mission from the lengthy version that sounded like every other corporate mission statement:

> 'KPMG shall be the world's leading accounting and consulting firm. We shall achieve this by delivering the highest quality services that provide significant added benefits to our clients and that meet or exceed their expectations. We shall thereby build enduring relationships and be always worthy of our clients', our people's and society's trust'

to the more inspiring – and memorable:

> 'KPMG is the global advisory firm whose aim is to turn knowledge into value for the benefit of its clients, its people and its communities.'

In addition to this, Colin had put some thinking into what resources KPMG could employ to achieve this mission. This may not sound like rocket science, but it is often the simplest concepts which are the most valuable in focusing any strategic developments and this is definitely true in this case. Deep down, Colin must still be an accountant, for he thought about this question in terms of KPMG's *assets* (which beats liabilities as a starting point!). He concluded that to achieve its new mission, KPMG could draw on three classes of assets. All three were equally important, and all were interdependent. They are:

- Clients
- People
- Knowledge

Each asset needs to be invested in, maintained and appreciated for its own intrinsic value. Interdependencies need to be understood and a balance maintained. For example, there is no point in investing only in winning new clients and in building client relationships if we do not develop our people to work with those clients. There is little point in developing our people if their learning remains locked up in their heads and is not added to the knowledge of the firm as a whole. And we can have the best knowledge management system in the world, but what use would it be if we could not populate it with the knowledge we gain from working with our clients? And so on. The interdependencies are too numerous to mention here. Identifying these three assets, the maintenance of which always needs to be held in balance, led people to realise that in the future KPMG's people and knowledge have to be considered as well as client needs. While it was recognised that this would give rise to constant dilemmas, it was clear that only through reconciling such dilemmas all three things: clients, people and knowledge, would prosper. This makes the manager's role a bit of a juggling match and at a later stage we actually made sets of juggling balls with 'clients', 'people' and 'knowledge' written on them. It's hard to keep all the balls up in the air, but if you drop one the show is over.

Our new mission statement would eventually be supported by a simple expression of three core values: 'We are passionate about working with our **clients** to deliver exceptional value. Our **people** flourish and realise their full potential. We continuously extend the frontiers of our shared **knowledge**.' There are many providers of professional advisory services, but I'm not aware of any similar firm which expresses its vision in terms of key assets: clients, people and knowledge.

At this point we paused to look at how far we had come. We had a clear understanding of KPMG's existing culture throughout the world. We also had a newly articulated statement of purpose to guide us. And we had the concept of our three assets: clients, people and knowledge, which would later become invaluable in focusing our strategy and culture change effort. All in all, we knew where we were starting from. We were now ready to enter into the next phase of the values process, which was to decide where we wanted to go.

Phase 2: Defining the Desired Culture

As we researched the existing culture, we did, of course, gain a sense of some of the things which people wanted to change. We had also been formulating the business case for culture change and this too had given rise to some suggestions. Now it was time to focus our efforts on defining more exactly the culture we wanted to move towards. Focus is the key word here. Anyone who has ever tried asking people to define their desired culture will know what I am talking about. If you throw out an unstructured question like 'What sort of culture do you want?' to a group of people, you will be bombarded with all sorts of ideas and wishes which are impossible to align or interpret. And it would serve you right, because you should know better by now. A common framework and some structure is needed to focus the discussion.

We needed to paint a vivid picture of the culture that we wished to move towards. To ensure that this picture was clear, we needed people to describe what sort of behaviours they would see – and not see – in the new culture as well as formulating a statement of the values we would wish to have at its core. But we also needed to ensure that all this tied in with the strategy and activities of our organisation. We needed to move away from the wish-list-brain-dump approach so often adopted in defining desired cultures and focus the discussion on something relevant and real. This is where Colin's gem about KPMG's assets came in very handy. If our firm stood or fell with these three assets: clients, people and knowledge, then it seemed to me that our values should reflect this. So from this point on, any work we asked people to do on the desired culture always focused on the themes clients, people and knowledge.

Reading this, you might feel that restricting the discussions to these three themes was too limiting or exclusive in what needed to be a creative process. In fact, the opposite was true. Because people had a focus to their discussions, the quality of what they produced improved dramatically. Discussions moved away from the meandering, shopping-list mode to something worthwhile, well thought through and useful. People often get caught up in discussions about what they should be discussing, rather than discussing the issues, and we had effectively removed that confusion.

There is another point to be borne in mind when it comes to formulating a statement of values. Values statements need to be concise and this is a further reason to focus discussions on a few, key themes. The number of core values in an organisation's culture is by definition very small – certainly not more than five. This should be taken into account when articulating the values statement. Some of the values statements I have heard from my clients (and also from within KPMG when we had so many different statements to choose from) are simply too long. They are too wide-ranging to represent the company's true values and are unfocused and hard to recall. I remember being at a student party in Belfast at about 3am when we were trying to recall the names of the seven dwarfs. It seemed important at the time. The conversation went something like this:

'Happy, Grumpy, Dopey . . . ah . . . Dozy?'
'No, no, no: Sneezy . . . Sleazy? . . . Doc? Spock?'
'Prancer, Lancer, Dancer . . .'

And this is when we were supposedly at the height of our intellect. Very few human beings can remember a list of more than five things. Three is even better. We didn't want people in KPMG to be stumbling over the values statement like a bunch of drunken students trying to recite the names of the seven dwarfs. The values statement needed to be memorable if it was going to be of any use, and that meant it needed to be focused and concise.

We had picked a few events to use in developing the desired culture. These events were very different in character. The first two events were development programmes ('training course') and the second was KPMG's International Partner Conference (which at that time was another word for 'jolly').

August/September 1997:The Bürgenstock Programmes, Switzerland
Every year in late summer, KPMG senior managers and partners from all over the world meet in a heavenly location in Switzerland for a rolling programme of seminars which promote global awareness. The seminars are geared towards high flyers – people who make key contributions to firm's global business. The programmes have always been a means to disseminate KPMG's international strategy as well as serving more general development purposes, and time is always allocated on the programme to enable participants to think about strategic issues in the firm. The programmes were therefore an obvious choice of event for the continuation of the values process. The difference was that this time, instead of commenting on existing strategies, participants were being asked to actually become involved in the strategy development process by working on the 'live' development of KPMG's desired culture.

Each programme that year was kicked off with a presentation of KPMG's strategy at its current state of development (no gloss) by Colin and Don Christiansen, who was then the firm's International Executive partner. Participants were asked first to work on their understanding of the statement of core purpose, and then to turn to the subject of values. Participants formed working groups for the duration of the seminar and it was the task of each group to take one of the themes of clients, people or knowledge and work on a thought-provoking brief. The brief asked them to think about how one particular asset (i.e. clients, people or knowledge) was valued at present in KPMG. They then had to look ahead, bearing in mind our purpose, and develop their thinking on what the firm's culture ought to be like. They assessed what needed to happen in order to bring about the changes they suggested and began to define, at a high level, 'how we will know when we have got there'. They also reflected on what they themselves would need to do to behave in accordance with the culture they were proposing.

> In August 1997, close to 200 people from KPMG worldwide gathered in Bürgenstock to develop the core values that would be the basis for the firm's new culture. The process was creative – one team even composed a song to explain their priorities. Many were thrilled to see that, at last, 'An opportunity had arrived to do something that could make a difference.' Despite a few dissenting voices, most agreed that change was necessary. Many felt that change was needed even sooner than planned.

They had been told that they could report back at the end of the week in any way they pleased. Their final presentations were very inspired – ranging from straight-talking sessions to theatre productions and songs. (It's amazing what people will do sometimes when they inhale that pure mountain air.) They generated ideas too numerous to mention here, and no summary can do justice to their work:

- On *clients*, they focused primarily on two things. Firstly, they looked at the nature of the client relationship. They acknowledged that KPMG is already good at this but they too felt that we were sometimes not challenging enough to clients. They wanted the client relationship to look more like a peer relationship, characterised by mutual respect, joint teams, sharing of ideas and solutions, openness and frankness. They also wanted to build closer and more lasting relationships with clients, which meant sometimes sacrificing short-term gain in order to maintain integrity and build trust and understanding. One group drew an analogy with a one-night stand versus a marriage, thankfully regarding marriage as the infinitely preferable type of relationship. The second point about clients was to do with the value which KPMG brings to the client organisation. They envisioned a KPMG in which everything we did added superior value. This meant, they said, that there may be some more routine work which we would have to stop doing, as well as developing new services which added more value.

- On *people*, again there were two key themes. One was about creating an environment where people were valued and respected. They described in great detail what this actually means in terms of behaviour. The second point was about development: they wanted KPMG to be world-class in ensuring that people got the best out of themselves, both personally and for the firm.

- *Knowledge* was viewed as the area where KPMG needed to improve most. In any culture change we undertook, participants said that knowledge sharing, becoming a learning organisation and ensuring that our knowledge was valuable and relevant, should be key priorities. At that time, KPMG had not yet developed its state-of-the-art knowledge management system, and our technology for knowledge sharing was far behind that of our competitors. However, the people at Bürgenstock pointed out that it was not only vital that KPMG acquired the latest technology, it was just as important that we changed our attitude.

Working on the values captured the imagination of the groups at Bürgenstock. They had plenty of other things to say besides talking about what the new culture should look like. They spoke a lot about commitment, recognising that change needed to happen on a personal level, and that each individual in KPMG needs to take responsibility for making it happen. In other words, participants were saying that it was not just the leadership who had to change: they themselves would have to change too. They stated categorically that KPMG should get tough on people who did not comply with the culture change, (even if it meant firing them), and pointed out that those who uphold the values should be visibly supported, protected and rewarded. They stressed the need for wide communication, and the importance of 'walking the talk'.

International Partners' Conference, San Francisco, September 1997
Historically, the annual KPMG International Partners' Conference was not renowned as being an event which involved hard work. The conference had the reputation of being a bit of a 'jolly': a well-deserved break from the strains of running an international business and a chance to catch up with colleagues from around the world. Typically, the three-day conference programme was fairly light, the entertainment programme magnificent and the locations generally chosen for their prime shopping, golfing and tourist attractions. Funnily enough (and I *genuinely* can't fathom this), a lot of the partners attending this event in the past had complained that it was boring. When Colin took over as International Chairman in February 1997, the conference, scheduled for September that year, was already in the early stages of organisation. The venue was San Francisco and Tony Bennett had been booked for the gala dinner. However, there were no ideas regarding the content of the programme, so what did Colin want to do? Colin wanted to radically change the nature of the event, turning it into a working conference. With many of KPMG's top partners from all around the world in one place, he reckoned that there were more useful things they could be doing than playing golf. He also wanted to introduce some sense of continuity with other events – the conference needed to fit better with KPMG's wider strategic programme.

The conference was held in mid-September. Around 350 KPMG partners from all over the world attended, curious to hear what the new Chairman would have to say. They had also been warned that this year's conference was going to involve them in doing some work. The first day of the conference was fairly traditional in its presentation style. The focus was very much on KPMG's globalisation strategy. Participants heard, among other things, about the need for globalisation, and how KPMG was going to achieve this with the 'virtual firm' strategy. The second day was devoted to working on two elements of the virtual firm strategy: values and core services. This was very much a working day, where the audience would no longer be an 'audience' but participants in the process in the true sense. The third day was set aside for reflection, review and looking forward. In the past, the conference had been a mecca for external speakers. This time Colin was adamant that people in KPMG would do their thinking for themselves, so only one guest speaker was invited. He spoke on the last day, and he didn't do a standard piece – he was interviewed live on stage and invited to share his own experiences and views on globalisation.

What all this meant for me was that I had 350 people for a half day as a captive audience to work on defining our desired culture, plus a little time the following day to clear up any messy bits. The main thrust of the work would be to paint a picture of the desired culture not just in terms of the values to which we aspired, but also the concrete behaviours which would support these values and enable us to change.

However, the 350 conference participants did not have the benefit of knowing what had gone before in terms of defining the business case or assessing the present culture. They were coming into the process completely cold, and before we were going to get any useful work out of them, we needed to be sure that they were familiar with what had already been discovered. Communicating the business case was easy. It was presented by Colin on the first day of the conference and it was touched on again before they started work on the second day. But we also needed to present our findings on the present culture and to be sure that the audience found them valid, and that was a more daunting task.

We were very conscious that we needed to present the current culture in a way which was clear, quick to assimilate and, while being honest, would not repel the audience or lead them into a state of self-flagellation. We hit on the idea of using drama to get the message across. We engaged a comedy script writer who, on the basis of the Hustler's Guide (when has any other corporate document been put to so many uses?), worked with us to write a series of sketches depicting a typical day in the firm, with all its foibles. Actors were engaged to take on the roles of KPMG employees, and they staged the mini soap-operas in the midst of the audience. While we were pretty confident that the sketches were a fairly accurate portrayal of KPMG at its best and worst, we needed to get a feel for whether the audience agreed, so the drama was interspersed with multiple-choice questions such as 'What would happen next?', 'How often does this happen in real life?', 'How many times has this happened to you?'. Each member of the audience was given an electronic keypad with which to respond. The sketches were hilarious but also realistic (so much so that one of the conference delegates mistook the actor who played the bumptious partner character for a real-life KPMG person). The whole show caused much amusement, but the serious outcome was that people were able to acknowledge the characteristics, good and bad, of KPMG's present culture. This was more validation for our research into KPMG's current culture, and it had the added benefit of warming up the conference participants to work on the next exercise.

The next exercise was to do some serious work on the values to which we aspired, and what this meant in terms of behaviour. There is a current fashion among change management consultants for something called the 'conference model', or 'large group intervention'. This basically involves getting a huge number of people who are representative of the whole organisation in a room together, working in real time on the issue, and assimilating their discussions, also in real time, into something sensible. Faced with the task in hand and 350 KPMG partners from all over the world to do it, the techniques of the conference model proved very useful.

Participants sat at tables of 10 in seats which had been pre-allocated to ensure 'max mix', i.e., maximum diversity. (In our case, this meant that we aimed to create as diverse a mixture of nationalities and functional expertise as possible at each table. We didn't want cliques of chums to sit together.) Each table had an appointed facilitator who had been briefed the day before and who would later act as the group's spokesperson. There was a very structured brief for discussion, and various pre-printed forms for recording each group's responses. The output of each group was collected and collated with that from other groups at various points in the discussion. After the discussions a further workshop was run just for the spokespersons, so that they could hear the views of other tables and agree the most important points. Three of the spokespersons were then selected to present on stage the views of the whole room and open discussions from the floor. The whole discussion process was a sort of cascade in reverse. In other words, having started with a wide range of inputs, messages were refined at each stage until the few most important points emerged at the end, with the essence of everyone's thinking being captured along the way.

> KPMG didn't launch its new values or vision until after we had genuinely consulted with people. It wasn't a case of: 'Here's our new values – what do you think?' Rather, we asked: 'What are the firm's values like now, and what would you prefer our values to be?' The amazing thing to me was how consistent the replies were across the worldwide firm. Everyone seemed to have a similar impression of where we were, what we should be aiming for instead, and what's most important to the firm's success.

I had done some training in the conference model that year and the one point that was really hammered home to us by the experts was that *logistics were everything*. The discussions, the timing and the collation of data all constituted a fine balance which had to be maintained or chaos would prevail. Quite true – it was vital to be well-organised. I had developed a finely honed process and there was an army of well-drilled people behind the scenes poised to collect and collate the data. It was infallible. Or it would have been, had I anticipated that fifteen minutes into the discussion the fire alarms sounded and the building was to be evacuated. I'm sure some of the non-native English speakers had their vocabularies enriched as they filed past me on to the street. However, we returned to the room after about fifteen minutes and by some miracle, everything worked out just fine. In fact, the incident seemed to lighten the mood and make for a better working atmosphere (not that I would recommend building it into the conference model methodology). And the San Francisco fire engine made great footage for the conference video.

Now for some detail about the content of the work. The room was divided into three sections (Tables were colour coded for easy identification). The discussions in each section focused on one of the themes of clients, people and knowledge. The brief consisted of two tasks:

- First of all, we asked participants to dream. They had to complete the sentence
  'I have a dream for KPMG's clients (people or knowledge) that . . .'
  In this way, we hoped to capture the highest aspirations of KPMG's leaders. I had a tremendous argument with one of the presenters, who felt silly asking such an off-the-wall question, and wished to rephrase it into something really inspiring like:
  'To succeed in the future, we at KPMG will need to focus on . . .'
  I won the argument (well, sort of – I got the other presenter to say it instead) and of course the Martin Luther King approach worked perfectly well with our international partners. Just because they are accountants, it doesn't mean they can't dream. The resulting statements of aspirations surprised even me with their intensity. It's not going too far to say that they were moving.
- Dreaming aside, the second task was much more focused on practicalities. If we were to achieve these dreams, what were the specific, identifiable behaviours which people in the audience and the rest of us at KPMG would have to stop, start and continue doing? The groups worked on generating huge lists of behaviours in each category. These lists have been perhaps the most valuable thing we ever did in terms of producing guidelines for behaviour and really helping people to visualise the culture we are trying to create.

So by the end of the San Francisco conference, we had an unedited list of several key themes and phrases for our lofty, inspirational values statement and a comprehensive, get-tough list of behaviours which we needed to stop, start and continue practising if we were to bring these aspirations to life. In all, I could not have wished for a richer picture of the culture which we now had to bring into being. We had also generated an interest in culture change with a large number of senior and influential KPMG partners from all over the world.

The rest of the conference had also gone extremely well. People were optimistic about the globalisation strategy. They appreciated the 'virtual firm' concept. They had participated in determining KPMG's core service offering. They had also enjoyed Colin's informal and no-nonsense style. It was looking good.

It was looking good until the last night of the conference. It was about 3am after the final gala dinner. Dazed by exhaustion, champagne and Tony Bennett's rendition of 'I left my heart in San Francisco', I was sitting in the hotel bar with some of my closest colleagues and a few mates from the conference production company. We had drifted into playing a game where we had to say what we thought each other's career would have been had we not all ended up doing what we were doing. I was just starting to get annoyed that each time it came to my turn, everyone seemed to be saying 'dental hygienist', and not, for example, 'management guru', when Colin wandered into the bar looking harrowed. He came over and told us that he had just heard the news that Price Waterhouse and Coopers & Lybrand, two of our major competitors, had just announced that they were merging to form the biggest and most powerful professional services firm in the world. So in the space of however long it took them to merge, we would slip from being among the biggest of the 'Big Six' advisory firms to being fourth out of five. Colin said:

'Oh well, the good thing is that at least the Council and the Board are all here already. We're meeting at 7am.'

Asia Pacific Regional and New Partners' Conference, Bali, October 1997
The fact that PwC (PricewaterhouseCoopers) was notably expand-

ing was enough reason for KPMG to focus even more on getting its act together globally. The values work had to go on, and with even more urgency than before.

Our statement of aspirations from the San Francisco conference still needed some refinement. We were scheduled to take the values proposition to the International Board in November to finalise the values statement and determine next steps, but in the meantime some prioritisation of the raw material from the International Conference had to be done. An item on the international agenda offered itself for this purpose: our Asia Pacific conferences took place at the perfect time to do this work, and offered a perspective from a group which had hitherto perhaps not been as involved as those from the more western reaches of KPMG. Besides, the conference was on Bali.

This is where I get upset. I had designed a very robust and engaging process to do this work with our Asia Pacific colleagues. I had also consulted my Lonely Planet guide and planned to unwind afterwards with a very enjoyable week-long trip around the island. Then, two days before I was due to fly to Bali, for no apparent reason, my right shoulder seized up altogether. I was in extreme pain and it looked like my conference session, not to mention my impromptu holiday, was in jeopardy. On the day I was due to fly, I spent half an hour on the phone to Colin in Bali, briefing him on how to run my session. I then went to Charing Cross Hospital in West London, where I was told by a sweet but incredulous rheumatologist that this condition didn't normally appear before age 50-60. On the day of the session, Colin prioritised our values themes with our best and brightest from the Asia Pacific region in a room overlooking a stunning, palm-fringed beach while I lay on a couch in rainy Kensington, being yanked around by a physiotherapist who brightly told me she had never seen such a severe case. Colin got some excellent input from the Asia Pacific partners, which I grudgingly included when I was putting together the material for the Board meeting.

One of the things which became very apparent during the Asia Pacific session was how important it is to be sensitive to local culture and language. For example, the raw material which was

KPMG's Asia Pacific practices met in Bali in October 1997 to provide a more international perspective on the values. It was there that I learned just how aware you need to be of local business cultures when creating something for a global organisation. As I presented themes for KPMG's new values, a number of people from the firm's Asian practices objected when I described our wish to establish 'peer' relationships with clients. At first I thought it was just a problem of language and that they were misinterpreting what I meant by the word 'peer'. But there was more to it than that. They explained to me that a 'peer' relationship between a supplier and a customer simply did not exist in their countries. No supplier, even if he was a company chairman, would be regarded as the 'peer' of a customer. In expressing an organisation's shared understanding, it is essential to see beyond language difficulties to the less obvious differences in culture.

used as input to the session talked about our need to develop 'peer' relationships with clients. Our Asian colleagues were adamant that this was a bad thing and when Colin, somewhat surprised, questioned them more closely, he realised that they were not objecting to the firm's intent to develop more *robust* relationships with clients, but they had a real problem with what they would term a 'peer' relationship. It did not fit with the traditions of respect in some Asian countries that an auditor or consultant would presume to call himself the 'peer' of the client. While it was not going to be an enormous effort to rephrase the values statement so that everyone would be happy with it, this incident did show how careful you need to be when working cross-culturally that shared sentiments are not confused by misunderstandings of local business practices or inappropriate use of language.

International Board Meeting, Miami, November 1997
By November 1997, I had assimilated the input from the entire process into a report for the International Board, who were to be responsible for the final crafting and approval of KPMG's global values statement. The report described the process in detail and summarised the key themes, aspirations and behaviours which

would be the basis for the final definition of our desired culture. The Board meeting would take the form of a workshop, at the end of which we hoped to emerge with our values statement. We also needed their commitment to a comprehensive implementation programme.

But the meeting didn't happen that way. The Board got distracted. Understandably so, because a few weeks before the meeting was due to take place, KPMG and one of our competitors from the Big Five accounting and consulting firms decided to join forces. We had announced on 20th October our intention to merge with Ernst & Young to form a professional advisory firm which would be far bigger than PwC. So our International Board had a few more urgent matters on their hands.

On Hold, November 1997–February 1998
Alas, just when we were on the point of agreeing the values and getting on with implementation, we had to put everything on hold. The whole process up to that point had focused, obviously, on creating something which was uniquely KPMG's, and now it looked like the organisation we had built all this for would cease to exist! Assuming all went to plan, we would have a new challenge: to integrate the cultures of KPMG and EY, or rather, to build something even better for the new firm. The problem was that during the negotiation process, no one could predict whether the merger would happen or not. There were tremendous regulatory problems, as well as the usual problems which hamper many merger negotiations. It was a strange time. On the one hand, it would have made sense to get a head start on building a common culture for the merged firm there and then. On the other hand, while the outcome was still uncertain, KPMG and EY were still competitors, with a more than outside chance of remaining so. Nor was there any point in KPMG pressing on to finalise its own values and do its own thing – what if that all had to be abandoned in a few months' time if the merger was finalised?

As time progressed, we began to feel more and more optimistic that the merger would go ahead, and the prospect of building a new culture in a new firm seemed more like an opportunity than a hassle. However, on Friday 13 February 1998, a disgruntled Colin called the team into his office to tell us that EY had suddenly pulled out of the negotiations. They had decided they didn't want to marry us after all. Although this was tremendously disappointing, Colin didn't waste time. He wanted to act fast to utilise the positive aspects of the situation. KPMG was reeling and indignant, and he knew that this would create a sense of urgency and a momentum for change which we could use to our advantage. Secondly, during the negotiations, we had learned a lot about our strengths and weaknesses, and it was clear what our priorities should be. The immediate priorities were to accelerate the 'virtual firm' strategy, to invest in building a world-class knowledge management system and to finally face up to the structural changes which would have to be made at an international level to enable us to globalise faster.

Finalising the Values Statement, International Board, Miami, March 1998

The time to agree KPMG's global values statement had finally come. At the highest level, the values consist of three simple statements. These statements have been carefully chosen to be lofty and inspirational, but also to reflect truly the aspirations which people felt to be most important. We wanted to be sure that people would understand clearly what the values meant in real terms, so as well as agreeing the high-level statement, the Board approved a short description of key elements which underpin it. We reproduce both here:

KPMG's Global Values:

We are passionate about working with our clients to deliver exceptional value

which means:
– being passionate about client service
– robust, lasting relationships
– being committed to adding value

Our people flourish and realise their full potential

which means:
– respect, support and trust
– adding value to our people by providing varied, challenging and
  rewarding work and planned career development
– teamwork: self-fulfilment through working and growing together

We continuously extend the frontiers of our shared knowledge

which means:
– openness of mind and continuous learning
– treating knowledge as a highly valued asset
– everyone in the firm has a right and an obligation to access our
  knowledge base, and the responsibility to contribute to it.

I mentioned earlier that we wished to preserve what was good about
our existing culture. We did not ignore the current culture when
defining the desired culture. Its positive qualities are reflected and
built upon in the new values statement. For example, the notion of
'the client comes first' has been modified and broadened to describe
a relationship which is much more robust and concerned with
adding value. With regard to our people, we acknowledge that
KPMG will always be individualistic, and the desired culture will
offer individuals ample opportunities to realise their full potential,
which is more possible in a supportive environment than a
competitive one. Our technical excellence and professionalism will
be maintained as part of our exceptional value offering to clients, as
well as being included in the learning which we offer to our people.
And our integrity, still key in building robust and lasting
relationships with our clients, is also present in the respect, support
and trust which we will foster within the firm.

   Reviewing where we had got to at this point: we had a statement
of values for the global firm. We knew what the values meant in real
terms. Not only that, we also had supporting definitions of the types
of behaviour which would support or undermine the values. All in
all, we had a rich picture of the culture we wanted to create.

> The people at KPMG are clever, well-educated individuals, with more than their fair share of worldly wisdom – so I expected a certain amount of cynicism in response to well-meant phrases such as 'shared values' and 'frontiers of shared knowledge'. To my surprise, there was very little cynicism. What avoided it, I think, was linking our culture change to an opening up of relationships and communication channels. Cynicism is the product of limited choice, and the effect of our process was to minimise it.

Now all we had to do was implement it.

Phase 3: Implementation

The subject of implementation is a chapter in itself, and for that reason Chapter 4 devotes itself entirely to this issue. But in the meantime, here are a few points we were facing at KPMG when we got to this stage.

KPMG has a poor track record of implementation when it comes to internal projects, because client work takes precedence. At this point in the process, we knew that whatever we did, we had to try extra hard to maintain momentum. We had to make implementation interesting, or, even better, make it enjoyable.

There were many initiatives in place at an international level which would help bring about culture change. As far as possible, these initiatives were integrated fully into our international organisational development programme. But we knew that if culture change was really going to happen in KPMG, then it needed to happen at a local level. Each national practice would have to make changes in line with the new culture. Now there's a mammoth undertaking for you. It clearly was not one which could be run by a few people in International Headquarters.

We had to make sure that people took ownership of the implementation at a local level. And we had to give practical assistance to make sure the culture change was achievable within the constraints which existed in the firm. At the same time, the approach we proposed had to be flexible enough to allow national practices to do things in their own way. It also had to accommodate the fact that some member firms had already carried out culture change programmes while others had not, and that all had different needs, different levels of sophistication and different local sensitivities. In other words, it looked like since we had 160 practices around the world, we would need about 160 culture change programmes, each tailored to local needs and each quite different, even though the goal, which was to build a corporate culture based on KPMG's global values, was the same. It was a case of many roads leading to Rome, but people locally would know better than we did what sort of road they should build.

> Although KPMG now has a unique, meaningful and inspiring set of core values, words alone are not enough. Indeed the meaning of those words would be interpreted differently by different organisations. More important than any particular expression of values is whether they are truly shared across the firm. It is the co-operative development and consistent practice of its values – not the values themselves – that gives the organisation a sense of purpose, a revitalising energy, and the will to succeed.

These were all good reasons for not adopting a rigid, dictatorial approach. Besides, we had been around in KPMG long enough to know that you can't tell people in the firm what to do. The answer to the implementation dilemma was therefore to develop something which was *enabling* rather than prescriptive, and which allowed local practices a great deal of flexibility in designing their own, unique culture change programmes. In other words, we needed to give people not a standard approach, but the tools and techniques which they would need to put together with their own approach. We decided to develop a 'values implementation toolkit', which would provide local practices with guidance, a framework and a selection of tools and techniques for bringing about culture change. People could pick out of the toolkit the things which best suited their own purpose, and adapt and add to it if necessary. By giving people a common set of tools rather than dictating a common approach, we could achieve alignment while maintaining flexibility and local ownership.

The senior partner of each of KPMG's national practices became responsible for implementing culture change in his or her own part of the firm. The toolkit was provided, along with assistance from International Headquarters where necessary. The toolkit approach is one which certainly works in KPMG, and it could also be applied successfully in any other organisation which has the misfortune of having business units which do not like to be controlled from the centre.

'What do you put in a toolkit for culture change?' I hear you ask, as most people find it difficult to imagine producing anything tangible which would help bring this about. (Incidentally, this question did cross my mind more than once even after I had agreed to produce the kit.) Answering this question gives an insight into what practical actions can be undertaken in *any* culture change programme, whether a toolkit approach is used or not, so the content of the toolkit, and the reasons why we put it together the way we did, are described in the next chapter.

Chapter 4

USEFUL TOOLS

Imagine you are a change agent about to embark on a programme of major change in a diverse organisation. A *'change agent'*? You have probably heard this bit of management consulting jargon before. While it conjures up exotic images of James Bond, it is in fact the term for the less than glamorous role of the person who is responsible for planning and implementing changes to an organisation on a day-to-day basis. I confess to finding the term 'change agent' a bit ridiculous, and I can never bring myself to say 'I'm a change agent' when someone asks me what I do for a living. However, since I haven't thought up a better word, we will just have to stick to it.

This chapter aims to help change agents at a very practical level. Although the focus is mainly on culture change, many of the lessons apply equally well to other types of organisational change.

One of the first things a change agent needs to do is to be clear about roles and responsibilities. The first part of this chapter looks at various roles in the change process, and what the people in those roles need to do to be effective. Much of this is received wisdom which can be applied to any change process or big project, but it is worth mentioning here as it is key to success that people understand their roles and fulfil them properly.

The second part of this chapter talks about practical tools and techniques which can be used to implement culture change. KPMG's values implementation toolkit is used as a basis for this, though I do not give an exact account of every single element contained in the kit. (With an implementation guide and thirty-six different tools, some of which are very KPMG-specific, I doubt if that would make the most riveting reading.) Instead, I describe in more general terms the content, and the motivations and principles behind the development of particular tools, as well as my experiences of using them. In this way, I hope to answer the question 'What do you put in a toolkit for culture change?' in a wider context than just KPMG's.

What is a change agent?: Roles in the change process
The change agent role is often misunderstood. It is frequently confused with other roles in the change process, and this can cause serious problems. There are also further, essential roles which need to be clearly defined and adequately fulfilled. Otherwise the change process is doomed to failure (this really is that important!)

Perhaps one of the simplest and clearest definitions of roles in the change process is that put forward by an American management consultancy called ODR as part of their methodology for managing organisational change. Many change managers still use their framework today and the following definitions derive from their work.

We recognise four roles in the change process:

1. *Sponsors* are the people who have the power to bring about change. They are ultimately accountable for making change happen and they have the authority to bring it about. *Key* sponsors are those at the highest level of authority needed to bring about the change. They will typically be found among the leadership team of the organisation. (For example, the key sponsor in KPMG's culture change process was Colin.) Sponsors are sponsors by virtue of their position in the organisation. In other words, if no one at the highest necessary level of authority is prepared to champion the changes you are proposing then there is no point seeking out someone at a lower level to fulfil the key sponsor role. Sponsors who fulfil their role well are referred to as *strong*, while those who do not are termed *weak*. It goes without saying that key sponsors should be strong. In addition, sponsorship at levels further down the organisation should be built and strengthened in order to sustain the programme.

2. *Change Agents* are responsible for implementing the change on a day-to-day basis. They are the people who design and facilitate the change process. Part of the change agent role is to ensure that sponsorship is built and maintained, so they may need to challenge sponsors where necessary, or make interventions in the leadership process. However, it should be borne in mind that change agents *do not have* ultimate decision-making authority. That responsibility lies with the key sponsors. I am an example of a change agent, as it was my role to design and run KPMG's culture change process.

3. *Change participants* are the people who actually have to change as a result of the process. For example, in a restructuring programme, the change participants may need to change significant parts of their jobs and their reporting lines. In KPMG's culture change process, there was a vast number of 'change participants', as the organisational and behavioural changes which resulted affected pretty much everyone in the organisation.

4. *Advocates* are people who speak out strongly in support of a change, but do not have the authority to bring about that change themselves. Advocates tend to be far-sighted people who often see the need for change before it is spotted by others. If the advocates can convince a powerful sponsor to take responsibility for bringing about the proposed change, their efforts will not have been in vain. However, if no sponsor is found, the advocate role can be very frustrating. Most of us will at some time have seen (or been) a frustrated advocate for change – one of those passionate but powerless crusaders for good who either wear themselves out or end up leaving the organisation in a huff (usually to be proved right when it is already too late).

It is vital at the start of the process that change agents establish what their role will be. In particular, they need to be clear about their responsibilities and the degree of authority they carry. It is also vital that sponsors understand their roles fully and appreciate that there are certain things which they cannot delegate to the change agent.

An honest exchange of expectations needs to take place at the beginning of the process. Because confusion about roles can be a difficult issue in any change process, it is worth reflecting on it here for a moment.

The problem is that with anything but the simplest changes, roles will inevitably overlap. One person might find themselves fulfilling several roles at once. Sometimes this is a good thing. For example, your *key sponsor*, if you are lucky, might also be a strong *advocate* of change. These are two roles which complement each other well. However, some roles do not complement each other so well and in fact may represent conflicting interests.

To illustrate what we mean by role conflict, let's forget about corporate life for a minute and take an example from real life. Suppose you were going on a diet. Your partner may be the *advocate* of the change, saying 'You're too fat. You need to lose weight.' But since only you have the power and accountability to ensure that you lose weight, you become the *sponsor* of your weight loss programme. Your next move will probably be to appoint yourself as *change agent* for the programme. In change agent role you begin designing and implementing your diet. You plan what you will eat and how much exercise you will take. In the first few days, as you are an enthusiastic sponsor and an effective change agent, you will have no difficulty persuading the *change participant* (also yourself, as the person actually on the diet) to comply. However, a few days later, you, the change participant, get fed up with feeling hungry all the time. You become grumpy. You crave chocolate. The trouble is that you, the sponsor, and you, the change agent, also feel hungry, grumpy and in need of a chocolate fix. In sponsor role, you weaken. You, the sponsor, force you, the change agent, to rejig the diet plan. The next thing you know you've consumed about 7,000 calories in one afternoon. What went wrong? You were trying to fulfil too many roles at once.

Back in the corporate world, similar situations arise. In major changes, everyone – sponsors and change agents included – can find that they are also *participants* in the change. As we all know, it is easier to tell other people to make difficult changes than it is to change oneself. Culture change initiatives are particularly prone

Important

to this type of role conflict, as they require that most people in the organisation, but especially those in senior positions, change their behaviour. For example, it would be disastrous if the key sponsor of a culture change programme were to speak out passionately in favour of behaviour change, allocate resources and budget to that change, and then not make any effort to change his own behaviour.

Some overlap of roles is inevitable and cannot be avoided. The best you can do is be aware that role conflict exists, expect it and prepare for it by thinking about how you might coach people in that situation. Another measure is, as far as possible, to keep the change agent and sponsor roles separate. If these roles are fulfilled by different people, the change agent will be able to intervene if the sponsor is weakening. Let's go back to the diet analogy to explain this: suppose the change agent had been someone other than yourself – suppose you had gone to a health farm or Weightwatchers for example, and let their staff take care of the diet plan for you. Then there would have been someone to challenge your weakening sponsorship, and someone who handled the day-to-day implementation a lot more objectively than you. This would be much more effective than having the same person fulfilling both roles. This wisdom applies not only in the case of the diet, but also in most corporate change programmes.

In summary, some attention needs to be given to roles and responsibilities in the change process. The key sponsor and the change agent need to be clear about expectations, responsibilities and boundaries. An appropriate working relationship – one in which the change agent has licence to challenge the sponsor where necessary – needs to be established.

Tools and techniques for practical application
Sooner or later in the culture change effort you will finally reach a point where you actually have to start *doing stuff* to implement the new culture. You will have already completed the first two stages of diagnosing the present culture and defining the values and behaviours which are fundamental to the desired culture. The fun part will be over, and you will no longer be able to put off that thing

you have been worrying about all this time: making it real. The following section does not provide any advice on how to conduct the first two stages of the culture change process, as most of the techniques we used at KPMG have already been discussed in the first three chapters. We focus here solely on the final stage: *implementation*. And by the way, this can be fun too.

When we reached the implementation stage at KPMG, we chose a toolkit approach because it seemed to fit best with the nature of our culture, because it enabled local ownership of culture change initiatives, and because it addressed the situation we were facing, which was that our 160 practices around the world all had different needs when it came to planning a suitable programme. Not every organisation will be so big or so diverse in its needs that it will have to undertake a mass roll-out of a toolkit for implementing culture change, but the activities in which even very small organisations will need to engage are essentially the same as those proposed in KPMG's toolkit. So whether you are facing a situation like KPMG was in 1998, where you are tasked with the global implementation of new corporate values, or whether you are conducting culture change for a much smaller organisation, the key elements of what you need to do will be the same. Treat the following as an in-depth case study: look at the content of the toolkit and the thinking which underpins it. This will give you a broad framework, basic components and ideas for developing your own, unique culture change programme.

How the toolkit was conceived
We needed to help KPMG people all around the world to implement the global firm's values. We could not tell people exactly what to do, because they would know better themselves what would work in their own practices. Applying the old adage that you can give a hungry man a fish, but to solve his long-term hunger problem it would be better to give him a fishing rod and teach him how to fish, we realised that the best thing to do would be to give people a toolkit to build their own culture change programmes. The concept was easy. I even had a vision in my mind about how the toolkit would look: an ingenious little thing,

complete with a snazzy handle, that looked like a doctor's briefcase. What would go *in* the doctor's case, I was not so sure.

As it turned out, the final packaging for the toolkit was fairly conventional: it ended up as a sleek slip-case containing six folders. (Not that the designers didn't try their best with my completely impractical doctor's case idea. I still have several abandoned prototypes – monstrosities all – lurking somewhere in my cellar.) Fortunately we fared better when populating the toolkit with content. Each of the six folders contains extensive guidelines, materials, documents, workshop designs and exercises which can be used in the culture change process. The idea is that local change agents select the tools they need to carry out their programmes, adapting and adding to the content where necessary.

There were endless possibilities for what might go in the toolkit – too many, perhaps. It was a struggle to decide where to draw the boundaries. Knowing where to stop is difficult because culture change should permeate every part of the business. But if you try to put together a toolkit to address every part of the business it would take you a lifetime. You might also (deservedly) get the reputation for being a megalomaniac who wanted to take over everyone else's job. In the end, the toolkit we produced for KPMG included only tools which were deemed central to the culture change process. The development of related items, for example, HR policies and documentation, was left in the safe hands of the professionals in the firm's support functions.

Even within the boundaries of the culture change effort, we had to be selective about what we included in the toolkit. If we put too much in, people would not use it. (I assume that most people are like myself, that is, when presented with huge volumes of printed material they have an allergic reaction and end up not reading any of it.) On the other hand, too few tools would not give change agents enough choice in their approach. In the end, we supplied a kit with an implementation guide and thirty-six supporting tools, techniques and materials. This was clearly not going to be an exhaustive set of items which would address every conceivable situation. There are many items which could be added, and no doubt there are a few things in there which few people will use. But in general, the toolkit contains enough to equip most people with what they need to put together a basic programme of culture change.

Basic tools and a secret weapon
One of the things I like about writing this in retrospect is that the development of the toolkit looks very well thought through, academic and structured. Not at all like we were making it up as we went along. In fact, during its development, chaos theory applied. The sleek, ordered package which is the toolkit evolved from a hotchpotch of all the techniques my colleagues and I had ever used plus a selection of new inventions which I thought would be a good thing for . . . some reason. In the early stages, the toolkit consisted of an archive box of about fifty disparate, scrappy documents – the physical manifestation of a brain-dump. Finally my editor and designers forced me to bring some order into the chaos, and in the space of an afternoon, we laid all the documents out on the floor and began to look at how we might structure the final product. Assembling the tools and techniques by theme, we found that (miraculously, I thought) a clear structure emerged quite naturally. There were six obvious classifications for the tools in the kit, and, with the benefit of hindsight, I would say that these are the six key areas of activity in any culture change programme. The categories which emerged as if by magic from my archive box of miscellaneous tools were:

- *Implementation Guide*
- *Leadership Alignment*
- *Personal and Team Development*
- *Communications*
- *Managing the process*
- *Content*

Let's look at each very briefly, and get an overview of what they are all about before plunging into the detail in later sections:

The first thing every change agent needs is a basic outline of what to do. The first element of the toolkit is therefore an

Implementation Guide which provides a basic framework for the culture change programme. While at times I have been positively evangelical in saying that there is no precise cookbook for culture change, there *are* broad principles to be followed and a logical sequence of activities to be carried out. The implementation guide presents these in the form of a five-stage programme design. It also gives some background and theory and indicates where the remainder of the tools and techniques in the kit should be used.

The rest of the toolkit consists of five folders of tools and techniques:

1. *Leadership Alignment*, which is what the first box of tools sets out to support, is fundamental to the success of the process. In simple terms, the contents of this folder provide tools and techniques for building and maintaining sponsorship, particularly at senior levels. In other words, these tools help the change agent to build commitment with the leaders of the organisation, making sure that they actively sponsor the culture change and that they become effective role models. Leadership alignment is a critical component of *any* kind of major change in an organisation. Unless a sufficient number of the company's leadership team champion the change, all the research shows that the programme will fail.

2. We have already said numerous times that behavioural change is a key component of culture change. Materials and exercises to support behavioural change in individuals and teams are presented in the second folder: *Personal and Team Development*.

3. All the research shows that poor communication is a major cause of failure in corporate transformation efforts. While most people accept that communication is very important, nevertheless it is often the case that communications are poorly planned, half-hearted and lacking in creativity. The third box of tools, *Communications*, provides the change agent with planning guidelines, materials and creative approaches to getting the messages across.

4. Moving away from specific tasks to more general activities: culture change, like any other programme, needs to be effectively managed. We were aware that many of the people who would be using the toolkit might not be seasoned culture change managers. Not only that, even experienced change agents would need to conduct their activities in a way which was broadly consistent with the overall effort. Either way, there was a need to provide guidance on *how* to carry out various activities. The fourth box, *Managing the Process*, addresses this need, for example by providing methods for conducting research, designing and running events, measuring progress and so on.

5. The change agent needs to have a firm grasp of the concepts involved in the culture change process and a rock-solid understanding of the organisation's culture – existing and desired. The change agent needs to be the infallible source of information on the culture and the change effort, and to be able to explain these things clearly to others. In other words, he needs to know the content inside-out. The final box in the toolkit, *Content*, provides a set of materials which explain in depth the values, the theoretical background and details of various elements of the programme.

The secret weapon

Maybe there *are* lessons which change agents can learn from special agent James Bond. 007 always had something clever up his sleeve to get him out of sticky situations. He always had a quirky little secret weapon, which enabled him to outfox legions of baddies who had to make do with the usual, run-of-the-mill heavy artillery. At KPMG we too needed a secret weapon: something unexpected which would effectively inject energy into the implementation phase of the culture change process. We needed to capture people's imagination and renew their interest in culture change, just at that point when they thought the fun had stopped. Our secret weapon was a board game which helped people learn about the values and the benefits of a new culture as they played it. (It was also good fun to play.) The board game, which is described in more detail later, became the most sought after and most talked about part of the toolkit. It successfully kept values on the agenda and added to the appeal of implementation.

> To me the most interesting of all the tools in the Values Toolkit is the Values Game – a board game which, in the playing, reveals to players the beneficial effects of aligning with KPMG's new values. The game was first played by the firm's leaders, and then spread across the organisation. It was fascinating to watch how each player started out acting only for their own gain, and then gradually realised that working together to add value – by sharing people and knowledge – offered far greater rewards.

Not every organisation will choose to use a board game as a means of communicating its new values, but every change agent should think about what sort of unusual, high-impact secret weapon she might have, or creative or unconventional approach she might use, to keep the change programme lively.

More about what's in the toolkit
In this section we look more closely at the contents of the toolkit, drawing out key points and examining why certain elements were deemed important. Some items will require a lot of explanation while others will not be described in detail. At times I will also digress, get on various personal hobby-horses and raise issues which I feel have not been covered sufficiently elsewhere. In other words, what is described below does not always give equal weight to all parts of the toolkit or the culture change process. I have also tried not to make the descriptions of the toolkit too KPMG-specific. However, although individual tools might not be transferable to other organisations, the principles behind them are. Try to see the following sections as sources of ideas and examples from which to learn. The intent is to give you a general picture of what needs to happen to bring about culture change.

We consider each component of the toolkit in turn.

The Process:

Implementation Guide
The Implementation Guide provides the basic framework for the culture change process. The guide is the change agent's Bible: a handbook to be referred to throughout the programme.

The introductory chapters of the Implementation Guide are a shortened version of the first few chapters of this book. In other words, they contain theory about values and culture as well as a history of KPMG's culture change process. In this way, change agents are equipped with enough background knowledge to get started on implementation.

The remainder of the guide gives a high-level design for the implementation programme and lists activities to be carried out at various stages as well as the tools and techniques which support these. We focus here on the programme design which is proposed in the guide. This design could easily be replicated by other organisations.

The framework for the programme design is a five-stage process supported by three ongoing activities. It is outlined in Figure 4.1.

Figure 4.1: *A programme for culture change*

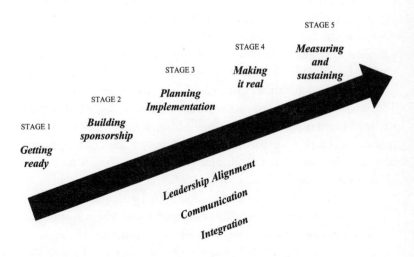

STAGE 5
Measuring and sustaining

STAGE 4
Making it real

STAGE 3
Planning Implementation

STAGE 2
Building sponsorship

STAGE 1
Getting ready

Leadership Alignment
Communication
Integration

Let's look at each stage of the process in turn:

Stage 1: Getting Ready
'Be prepared' is the girl guide motto. Actually, 'Semper paratus nunquam non paratus' is an old motto in my family. It translates as 'Always prepared, never unprepared'. In other words, my distant ancestors pinched their values statement from the girl guides but, being pedantic old so-and-sos, added a double negative at the end just to be sure to get the point across (another likely explanation is that they just had limited Latin vocabulary). Anyway, somewhere in my subconscious it must have sunk in, because the first stage of the implementation process I propose is for the change agent to *get ready* for what lies ahead.

Perhaps the most important thing for the change agent to do at this stage is work out with the sponsor what their respective roles will entail. We talked about the change agent and sponsor roles at the beginning of this chapter, emphasising how vital it is for both parties to be clear about their responsibilities and levels of authority. KPMG's situation was unique in that many new change agents were appointed specifically for the implementation phase of the process. In most organisations, the change agent will, by this stage, already have established a relationship with the sponsor. However, even change agents who have been involved in the previous phases of the culture change effort should consider reviewing the nature of the role, because the implementation phase presents new and different challenges from the initial stages of diagnosis and definition of the desired culture.

There are also a thousand other things to be done in this phase. This is an opportunity to gather information which is needed prior to implementation, as well as refreshing and revisiting research which was carried out in the initial phases of the culture change process. Here are a few examples of what else the change agent needs to think about:

- The change agent needs to become an infallible authority on the company's existing and desired culture. This requires some homework: the change agent needs to make sure that he can answer any questions which people might have about the company's values, what they mean in terms of behaviour, what will be changed, why it will be changed and how it will be changed.

- Attitudes to the culture change need to be sensed. Finding out how people feel about the culture change will aid tactical planning. Are they supportive? Or do they think it is all a waste of time? Do they really believe anything will happen? Taking this into account will enable the change agent to plan more effective interventions and communications.

- The politics and dynamics of the local situation need to be understood, and any additional research into the peculiarities of the existing culture carried out. In other words, the change agent needs to know for sure where she is starting from.

- Relationships need to be built with people who will be involved in the process. Culture change affects everybody, and the change agent will have to rely on a wide number of colleagues in support and management functions for help. There may also be a need to build relationships with people outside the organisation (for example, consultants, coaches or facilitators). The sooner the change agent can build constructive, collaborative relationships with such people, the better.

- Potential areas of resistance need to be investigated. It is natural for human beings to resist change. Even if their logic tells them they want the change, the emotional stress of actually having to do it will cause resistance. The change agent needs to work out where resistance is likely to be highest, and to plan how best to tackle it.

- Past successes and failures need to be investigated and learned from. It really is worthwhile finding out what worked well and what was a disaster in the past, because organisations, like humans, have a knack of repeating their old patterns. Some time spent talking to the wise and the scarred can be invaluable in helping to build on success strategies and avoid disasters.

- Data needs to be gathered for the all-important business case. By the time implementation comes round, the business case might already be in quite good shape. But it is important to make sure that it is always up-to-date and that it has been tailored with appropriate data to make it relevant to the audience. The business case will be fundamental in helping to build commitment among sponsors, so it needs to be compelling and convincing.
- The high-level approach to implementation needs to be developed (which is why the change agent will be reading the Implementation Guide in the first place) and any necessary resources need to be engaged.

In summary, there is plenty of preparation to do. And if you feel exhausted just thinking about it, note that this is all before the implementation process has even started!

Stage 2: Building Sponsorship

Many change programmes fail for lack of sponsorship. This is because sponsors often do not fully understand what their role entails, or because they were not truly convinced at the start that the change was necessary. This second stage of the implementation process focuses on building sponsorship.

Of course, once sponsorship has been built, the job is not finished. Sponsorship is a fragile thing and has to be carefully and constantly maintained. It is hard to determine where the building of sponsorship ends and the maintenance of sponsorship starts. And it is equally tricky to represent these two on a programme plan. You will therefore find that many of the activities outlined in this second stage of the process overlap with the ongoing process of *Leadership Alignment* which is described later. In fact, for much of the time, the two processes are the same. My advice is not to worry so much about where you are on the diagram (Am I 'building sponsorship' or 'aligning leadership'?), but just to make sure you do it. It's very, very important.

However, there are a few steps which clearly belong to this stage of the programme. The first is to work out who the sponsors are.

Identifying key sponsors is fairly obvious – they will be found primarily among the leadership team. However, there may also be a few people with significant influence and authority outside of the leadership team, and it is essential that you gauge in how far their sponsorship will be needed. There is also the matter of managers further down the organisation whom you will need to help sustain sponsorship as the programme continues. Particularly in large organisations, where the CEO might be a fairly remote figure, most staff pay attention to what their immediate boss says. If, for example, a middle manager does not support the change herself, then all the staff within her sphere of influence will be discouraged from supporting it (or, at best, not encouraged to support it). Often, the drive for change which comes from the leadership team dissipates halfway down the organisation because of weak sponsorship at those levels. To counteract this, the change agent needs to identify areas in all parts of the organisation where sponsorship needs to be built, and to take action to ensure that sponsors throughout the ranks are engaged in the process.

The problem with sponsors is that there is not much choice about who they are: sponsors are sponsors just by virtue of their position and they cannot escape this role. It has already been pointed out that sponsors may be strong or weak. Needless to say, the change process will only succeed if sponsorship is sufficiently strong. The change agent needs to assess this early on in the process. Most people can find out how strong sponsorship is likely to be by simply talking to those concerned (though the toolkit also provides a questionnaire for this purpose). Some of the questions to be asked of sponsors are tough. Is the sponsor sufficiently dissatisfied with the present situation? Is he clear about what will be achieved by implementing the new culture? Does he understand the further ramifications of the programme? Is he willing to allocate resources, give his public support, and be consequential about whom he rewards and reprimands? Is he willing to change, personally, in line with the new culture? What sort of priority is he giving to the culture change, in comparison with other activities which he may be sponsoring? All these questions will help determine the strength of a particular sponsor.

Only a very lucky change agent will find that sponsorship is perfect from the very beginning. Inevitably, sponsorship will be weaker than hoped. In this situation, there are a few choices to be made:

- The change agent could give up, though this is clearly not the preferred option. In cases where sponsorship is hopelessly lacking, terminating or postponing the programme may in fact be the best thing to do. If, for example, even the key sponsors are not prepared to give the programme their full support, then it is better to give up than to enter into a culture change programme which is doomed to fail (thus undermining the credibility and chances of success of any future programmes). If circumstances are really this dire, be brave and say so. Besides, saying something can't be done is usually a great motivation for people to prove you wrong.
- The more likely scenario will be that sponsorship is patchy. You may have some enthusiasts, but you will also have more than a few cases of lukewarm interest. What do you do with weak sponsors? Well, you could ask your key sponsor to fire them all and appoint strong sponsors in their place. Or you could do the decent thing and give them a chance. Giving them a chance means working with them and coaching them to build their effectiveness as sponsors. This is where *Building Sponsorship* and the ongoing process of *Leadership Alignment* overlap. The *Leadership Alignment* section of this chapter describes the various interventions and techniques which can be used to get the leadership team (or any other community of sponsors) fully on board with the change.

Stage 3: Planning Implementation

Culture change is all about making organisational and behavioural changes which support the company's desired values. In practical terms, this means that initiatives geared towards these organisational and behavioural changes need to be planned and implemented.

First of all, areas for change need to be identified and prioritised. This should cover both organisational and behavioural changes, but the key word is 'prioritise'. Focus should be maintained on the few activities which will make the most difference. There is often a temptation to do too much, but this is not a good idea. We have all at some point experienced the sheer stress in organisations caused by 'initiative overload', that is, too many projects going on at once. Few change agents will be starting with a blank slate. Every organisation will already have a range of projects underway, and these should also be taken into account when planning new initiatives.

The range of organisational changes to be undertaken will vary from company to company. At KPMG we encouraged people to think first about the values of our desired culture and the behaviours we are trying to create, and then to look at how the various artefacts of our culture needed to change to support these. Sometimes the changes to be made were obvious: for example, KPMG's purpose and values show a great commitment to the firm's knowledge base. In the past, the firm's knowledge management systems were inferior to those of our competitors. Now, as a result of huge investment and the commitment of people all over the firm, KPMG has a knowledge management system which is second to none. Another example from KPMG is that HR processes have been changed to support our new values. Both these examples are classical organisational changes which can be undertaken to support a new culture. Of course scope for organisational changes goes beyond systems and processes. It is also worth looking at how other artefacts of the culture might be changed, for example, symbols, rules and myths. Who gets recognised and who gets overlooked? It is often changes to these more subtle elements of the culture which convince people that there is true commitment to change.

Behavioural change initiatives need to go hand-in-hand with organisational changes. Behavioural change initiatives require a high degree of sensitivity in their management. There are all sorts of approaches which can be taken, varying from large group events to individual and small team coaching. The correct approach depends very much on the 'style' of the organisation in question. At KPMG, we carried out a full range of activities, from conferences to personal development activities. More detail of the latter is given in the section entitled *Personal and Team Development*.

In conclusion, this third stage of the culture change process is all about developing high-level plans. Objectives need to be set and broad time-frames agreed. A change strategy needs to be developed: decisions need to be made about the management style to be adopted and the numbers and types of people involved.

Stage 4: Making it Real

I suppose this is stating the obvious: now that all the initiatives have been planned you actually have to *do* them.

Stage 5: Measuring and Sustaining

As the programme proceeds, progress will need to be assessed. This can be achieved through applying various quantitative measures (a few of which are contained in the toolkit) as well as conducting less formal reviews and discussions.

The culture change process needs to be flexible to take into account new needs and opportunities which arise. At various points, the change agents, project managers and sponsors should take time out to refine the approach.

Learning from the process needs to be captured and integrated into the planning of future activities. It is also time to celebrate successes, and to ensure that motivation is maintained.

Ongoing Supporting Processes

As well as the five stages of implementation, there are three processes which support the change programme throughout its duration. They are:

- *Leadership Alignment*, which is critical to every stage of the process. The leadership team's effectiveness as sponsors is built and maintained through this process. Approaches to achieving leadership alignment are described in the relevant section below.

- *Communication*, which is one of the more important, but usually most neglected processes in any change programme. Communications need to be planned and executed as a fully integrated part of the change programme, not as an after-thought or add-on. Tools and techniques are described later in this chapter.
- *Integration*: The aim of a culture change programme is to embed a shared set of values in *every* part of the organisation. The new culture should become second nature, all over the organisation. The new values should be inherent in the normal corporate agenda. Because of this, you will know you have succeeded when there is no longer any need for a separate 'culture change initiative'. It should be the aim of every change agent to integrate their activities with the man-agement and infrastructure functions of the organisation as early in the process as possible. Change agents need to liaise closely with their colleagues throughout the organisation, to attempt to work with what exists already (rather than starting up competing initiatives) and to ensure that their activities complement what is being done. Not only does this save time and effort, it also helps change agents make friends with people whose support they really will need as the programme moves forward.

A note on real life

The framework for culture change presented in Figure 4.1 looks delightfully simple. It has clear, sequential stages and well-defined activities. Of course this is nothing like real life. In reality, all sorts of constraints and opportunities arise to complicate the process. In addition, as the programme progresses, the change agent will need to repeat parts of the process with groups beyond the leadership team. Various activities will need to be cascaded throughout the organisation to different target groups. Change agents may there-fore find themselves managing activities from all of the phases at once. It sounds chaotic but this is normal. There is a rule which change agents should always bear in mind: if you think it's easy, you're missing something. However, having a framework in mind, particularly if real life looks messy, will help you manage the chaos – and yourself.

The Tools:

Leadership Alignment
Leadership alignment is an essential part of culture change. When we say 'leadership alignment' what we mean is that the senior people in the organisation: the leadership team, your key sponsors, are fully supportive of the new culture and the change programme. To make sure that the leaders of the organisation think and behave in this way, the process aims to:

- ensure that leaders fully understand the values and are able to articulate them to others in an inspiring way,
- ensure leaders are fully committed to implementation,
- help leaders to role model the behaviours which the new culture requires, and to instil these behaviours in others.

Faced with a real-life leadership team, this sounds more than a little demanding! Fortunately the activities to achieve this nirvana-like state break down into five more manageable steps. The tools and techniques which are included in KPMG's toolkit for this purpose are too specific to reproduce here, but what is useful is to look at the more general goals which they support. The goals of the leadership alignment process will be broadly the same for any culture change, irrespective of the organisation, and can be used for guidance as the change agent puts together a programme of workshops, Board sessions, one-to-one coaching or whatever.

The five goals are (not necessarily in this order):

1. *Leaders need to truly understand the company values, and be able to articulate to others what they mean. They need to be able to paint a clear and inspiring picture of the desired culture to the rest of the people in the organisation, including what the values mean in terms of behaviour.*
Even though the leadership team will have been heavily

involved in developing the values, they may even now not have a common understanding of what the new culture really means, or they may not have thought in depth about some of the tough choices which they will be required to make. They may also struggle with how best to communicate their picture of the new culture to others. The change agent can help them through coaching and discussion, as a team or individually.

2. *The leadership team needs to show commitment to implementing the values. Members of the leadership team need to be able to present a compelling case for change to others in the organisation.*

   The leadership team needs to truly believe that the new culture will make a difference. Their commitment can best be gained by building a sound business case in which they all believe. The best way to help people buy into a business case is to involve them in developing it. It needs to be a business imperative, not just a 'nice to have'. And there needs to be a sense of urgency – is this something which needs to happen right now or can it wait? Leaders in organisations have enough to worry about without concerning themselves with non-urgent projects which may or may not be vital to business performance. If they are not convinced themselves, they will have trouble convincing others. A leader who passionately believes in the importance of values and culture change will be the greatest asset a change agent can hope for. We have a number of leaders in KPMG who passionately believe in our organisation's values, and it is not surprising that their practices have made astonishing progress in culture change.

3. *Members of the leadership team need to become effective role models of the desired values and behaviours.*

   The leadership team needs to support the new culture in words *and* deeds. Everyone will be watching them to see whether they themselves actually exhibit the behaviours they advocate. Role models such as those on the leadership team are the last people who can afford to fail at behavioural change. Behavioural change is difficult, so even if the leadership team are in pretty good shape, a great deal of work needs to be done. The change agent can organise feedback, coaching, mentoring and team sessions for the leadership team. No one can radically change their behaviour overnight, but by openly undertaking personal development activities, the leadership team can demonstrate their commitment to change. For example, in KPMG, a number of member firms introduced 360° feedback (more about what this is later) for all partners and senior staff. This broke the mould in terms of showing a commitment to behavioural change, and the credibility of the culture change programme (and the leaders) soared.

Once our aspired values were agreed, my role in KPMG's culture change process was to be a sponsor of the change – along with the other leaders of the international firm and the heads of the member practices. That sounds like an easy task, but sponsorship in culture change is not just a passive approval – it is a highly proactive promotion of the process. First, the sponsor must embrace and live the values personally, in order to set an example, and must then champion them visibly in every possible situation. For example, Mike Rake, who heads up KPMG in the UK, tirelessly and passionately promotes the values in words and actions. He has appointed some of our best organisational consultants to work on the culture change process full time, and has already instigated a string of successful, lasting changes.

4. *The leadership team sets objectives and priorities for the values implementation.*
   As sponsors of the change programme, the leadership team will be involved in defining the programme's overall goals and high-level activities. They will need to provide direction and support as the programme continues. This step in the leadership alignment process complements Stage 3 ('Planning Implementation') of the programme plan.

5. *The leadership team agrees plans for implementation, including measurement and communication processes.*
As the change programme progresses through Stages 4 and 5, the leadership team need to remain active in sponsoring the changes.

Personal and Team Development
The ultimate purpose of a culture change programme is to establish a new set of values as guiding principles for how people behave at work. A great deal can be achieved through making organisational changes (for example to processes, systems, rewards and recognition), but this in itself is not enough. To effect lasting culture change, you need to help people, at a personal level, to change their behaviour. Changing behaviour can be difficult, and the approach requires a great deal of skill and sensitivity, but the benefits both to the organisation and the individual can be enormous.

Most organisations already offer a suite of personal development programmes and any activities started as part of the culture change initiative should tie in closely with these. Change agents are advised to work closely with their colleagues in the HR function. At KPMG, many of the personal development activities suggested in the toolkit have already been absorbed into HR processes.

In the *Personal and Team Development* section of the toolkit, we focused on the few things which we felt would make the greatest contribution to values-driven behavioural change. Development activities are suggested both at an individual level and at a team level. For individuals, the goal was to make people more aware of their behaviour in relation to the values and help them change. For teams, the goal was to promote more effective teamworking and to ensure that the firm's values shaped how team members worked together.

Let's look at the types of things we put in this section of the toolkit and, more importantly, why.

Know Thyself
Changing behaviour at an individual level is not unlike changing an organisation's culture: The first thing you need to know is where you are starting from.

Most people profess to know themselves pretty well. No one can tell better than yourself if you are feeling happy, sad, bad-tempered or at peace with the world. The trouble is, while we all know exactly how we ourselves think and feel, we do not always know how *others* see us. Other people do not see our thoughts and feelings. They only see our *behaviour*. Even the most self-aware individual is likely to have blind-spots about their own behaviour. You can't change something you don't know about, so the first step in behavioural change is to find out from others how your behaviour is perceived.

In practical terms, the best aid to behavioural change is decent feedback. Feedback helps people become more aware of their behaviour and how it affects others. It often enables people to discover things about themselves that they would not normally see – both positive and negative. Feedback helps people to enhance their positive qualities and diminish negative ones.

Unfortunately most organisations, KPMG included, have a severe disability when it comes to giving and receiving feedback. Very few people look forward to feedback sessions, even though few would deny its value. The subject of feedback is addressed at great length in KPMG's culture change toolkit, and the very first item which people find when they open the folder is a set of guidelines for giving and receiving effective feedback.

The giving and receiving of effective feedback is material for an entire chapter of a book like this, and we reflect only on the basics here:

Giving feedback

Most people tend to home in on the more negative aspects of feedback, and the natural reaction to this is to become defensive. Sensitivity is required if feedback is to be constructive.

- Good feedback should be very specific, focusing on observable behaviours. The person giving the feedback should not try to interpret why the receiver of the feedback is behaving in a particular way. Feedback should be descriptive rather than evaluative: it should focus on events and not on the (imagined) character of the person. To give an example, it is OK to say to someone 'You interrupted a lot in that meeting', as this is an observable behaviour, but it is not very helpful to say 'You are really domineering', because how will the person know what they are doing, specifically, to make you think that?

- On the other hand, it is good to let people know how their behaviour affects you, but then you need to be clear that you are talking about *your feelings*, not the person's character. To take the current example a step further, it is fine to say 'You interrupted a lot during that meeting. I *felt* that you were being too dominant.' This gives the person specific feedback about what they did, and how you felt about it. It also gives them the opportunity to change their behaviour, for example, by keeping quiet next time.
- Feedback should focus on behaviours which the subject can do something about.
- The person giving the feedback should check for understanding.
- The time and the place should be appropriate.
- Feedback should be balanced: positive and negative, strengths and weaknesses.

Receiving feedback

How many of us look forward to feedback sessions? It can be difficult to take on board information about ourselves, but defensiveness blocks our ability to make use of feedback. Receiving feedback can be just as difficult as giving feedback, so here are a few more tips:

- Listen to *all* the feedback, keep an open mind and do not reject any of it straight away.
- Remember that feedback describes people's perceptions of you, not what sort of person you are.
- Don't just focus on the negative aspects of the feedback. Accept good feedback. Don't dismiss it as pleasantries.
- Don't try to think up excuses or justifications.

- Check that you have understood what the person is saying, paraphrasing or asking for further explanations and examples if necessary.
- If you are unsure about what you could do to improve negative behaviour or build on positive behaviours, ask the person giving you feedback for advice.
- Remember that most people find it difficult to give feedback. Say 'thank you'.

Another angle on feedback

Often, people only receive feedback from their boss at work, and this can give a rather one-sided picture. They do not have the benefit of knowing what those who work for them think. It is becoming more and more common in organisations for people to receive what is termed *360° feedback* as part of their personal development. In other words, they receive feedback from all directions: they find out not just what their boss thinks, but also what their peers and subordinates think of their behaviour.

KPMG's toolkit contains an instrument for administering values-based 360° feedback. It was developed on the basis of the lists of positive – and negative – behaviours which were defined way back in San Francisco, when the picture of our desired culture was painted. It enables people to receive very specific, purely qualitative (i.e. there is no scoring of boxes) feedback from a selection of superiors, peers and subordinates (some people have even sent the feedback form to clients). It has been widely and very successfully used.

At this stage, 360° feedback in KPMG is still carried out anonymously. In other words, although the subject chooses who will give her feedback, the comments gathered are not attributed to any one person (that is not to say that the recipient of the feedback does not indulge in guessing-games about who said what . . .). Clearly, an ideal organisation would be one in which feedback becomes a natural, spontaneous and valued part of daily interaction. However, few organisations have cultures which are open enough to sustain this, and in the meantime, an anonymous process is a good beginning. Good and honest feedback requires a safe environment, and all change agents should bear this in mind when introducing new feedback mechanisms. Even anonymous, 360° feedback can meet with resistance.

Changing the behaviour of individuals and teams

Feedback is key in raising awareness of what needs to change, but people also need some assistance in actually changing. The toolkit also contains a range of exercises which help people to make use of their feedback and plan their own programme of behavioural change. The key here is to provide people with choice. Some people might prefer to address the matter on their own with a personal coach, while others might prefer to work it out within a group context.

Teamwork is encouraged in KPMG's values system, so several exercises in the toolkit focus on team behaviour rather than individual behaviour. We included exercises (mostly facilitation and review processes for meetings) which are very specific to KPMG's values. We did not include any more general team-building or bonding exercises, not because these are a bad idea, but rather because there is already a multitude of excellent activities and games for this purpose in the public domain.

Communications

People often grumble about poor communication in their organisation. To even the most well-meaning project manager, communications can seem impossible to get right. In the toolkit, we supplied guidelines and materials to support the change agent in making the communication process as effective and painless as possible. We focused on providing support in four areas:

1. *Communications strategy* – Corporate communications are often planned and executed tactically rather than strategically. This is a polite way of saying that they are often carried out at the last minute and without much consideration of the message, the best medium and the audience. While external circumstances can often give rise to unexpected events which require reactive responses, there is no excuse

for resorting to tactical communications in a planned project. A substantial part of the communications section of the toolkit is dedicated to helping the change agent put together a well-considered communication strategy which is fully integrated with the rest of the culture change programme.

2. *Communications materials* – The toolkit provides presentations and handouts which tell the story of the values, explain what they mean, answer frequently asked questions and prompt discussion.

3. *Exercises which bring the values to life* – Conventional communications can only go so far in getting the message across. We needed to provide some things which would help people see how the values applied to them, personally, in their day-to-day working life. This included team exercises, the board game, and other tools, for example a 'values benchmark' to assess how well people are doing in putting the values into practice.

4. *Communication standards* – Consistency of communication is vital. The messages have to be clear and steps need to be taken to ensure they are not corrupted as they are passed around the organisation. With standard templates and guidelines, we ensured that the programme would have a consistent 'look' throughout the world. We also provided translation guidelines to ensure that the messages would not get misinterpreted.

Managing the Process
These are the tools which assist the change agent in the overall management of the programme.

This section of the toolkit addresses all those things which new change agents are dying to know but too shy to ask, including simple guidelines on how to conduct research, run workshops, use focus groups and conduct interviews. There are also presentations and notes which supplement the implementation guide in describing the more technical areas of change management.

A number of the tools in this section are less generic: these include interview formats, workshop designs and questionnaires which are specifically designed for KPMG's change programme.

The remaining tools in this section are provided to help the change agent measure progress. Guidelines and suggestions for developing qualitative measures are included as well as more specific survey questionnaires.

Content

The tools in the *Content* box help the change agent, and others, to understand in more depth some of the concepts which underpin the change programme as well as the desired culture.

Many of the concepts which the tools in this section set out to explain, such as the business case, roles in the change process, how to choose an appropriate change strategy or the theory behind corporate culture, have already been explained in detail in this book. But there is one item in this section which deserves some special attention here: it is a document which explains very clearly what KPMG's desired culture is all about.

At various points in this book I have stressed how important it is to paint a vivid picture of the desired culture. At KPMG we spent a great deal of time developing the statement of the values to which we aspire, and as well as that, the behaviours which support these values and those which, if continued, would undermine them. People also were asked to imagine how it would feel when we had 'got there': how would we know when the desired culture had come into being? All this thinking is summarised in this document, which we entitled 'Practising our Values' because that is exactly where it provides guidance. Rather than describing this in any more detail, excerpts from the document are given in Figure 4.2.

'Practising our Values' can be used by anyone who wants to understand more about the type of firm KPMG wants to be. It can be used as a basis for feedback, or simply for reflection. It helps people relate the values to behaviour in a very, very specific way.

Figure 4.2: *An Excerpt from 'Practising our Values'*

KPMG's mission is:

To be the global advisory firm whose aim is to turn knowledge into value for the benefit of its clients, people and communities.

To achieve our mission, we will focus on how we can grow, add value to, and best deploy our three key assets: clients, people and knowledge.

Supporting and complementing our mission are the three values which we aspire to have at the core of KPMG's culture.

OUR VALUES
- We are passionate about working with our **clients** to deliver exceptional value
- Our **people** flourish and realise their full potential
- We continuously extend the frontiers of our shared **knowledge**.

These values need to become the guiding principles for our way of working. They will be reinforced through organised processes and performance management systems, but it is also up to us as individuals to make a personal commitment to practising them each day.

The purpose of this document is to describe in more detail the behaviours which will uphold these values – and to alert us to current habits which, if continued, will undermine the values and the success of KPMG. Thousands of KPMG people from all over the world have contributed in an open and frank way to defining these behaviours. They should be relevant to all of us and it is a challenge now to each of us as individuals to change our behaviour in line with the values.

'WE ARE PASSIONATE ABOUT WORKING WITH OUR
CLIENTS TO DELIVER EXCEPTIONAL VALUE'

**Our client relationships are fundamental to our business. We
have always been good at building close and lasting
relationships with our clients and we have always focused on
client service. We now want to build on our strengths and
enhance the nature of our client relationships so that we
become trusted business partners who consistently add
value and exceed our clients' expectations.**

In essence, our client value means:

- Being **passionate** about client service
- Building **robust**, lasting relationships
- Being committed to adding **value**.

INDIVIDUALS WILL DEMONSTRATE THIS VALUE BY:

- Being proactive and energetic in their approach to client service
- Ensuring they understand the client's business
- Enjoying their contribution to the client's success
- Ensuring the client gets the right skills and resources,
  irrespective of discipline or territory
- Building relationships with clients characterised by mutual
  respect and openness
- Offering the client constructive challenges which take their
  thinking forward
- Listening to the client before formulating solutions
- Always meeting commitments
- Being exemplary in communicating with the client
- Being prepared to take short-term personal risks in the long-
  term interest of the client
- Focusing on providing those services to the client which truly
  add value.

KPMG WILL NOT TOLERATE INDIVIDUALS WHO UNDERMINE THIS VALUE BY:

- Avoiding uncomfortable client situations
- Keeping the client to themselves or 'protecting' them from other KPMG services or offices
- Giving advice based on standard solutions because they are easy or familiar
- Undercharging and/or overselling
- Being reactive rather than proactive or imaginative
- Always focusing on chargeable hours and not on added value to the client
- Always limiting the client relationship to the CFO
- Sacrificing long-term for short-term revenues
- Being afraid to challenge a client.

WE WILL KNOW THAT WE ARE PRACTISING THIS VALUE WHEN:

- Our clients choose us because we add the most value to their business
- Our clients find that working with our people is stimulating and enjoyable
- Our ability to acquire and retain clients far exceeds that of our competitors
- Our people feel that they are truly making a difference to their clients' businesses
- Our work and our relationships are valued so highly by our clients that we see significant improvements in our revenues and profits.

'OUR **PEOPLE** FLOURISH AND REALISE THEIR FULL POTENTIAL'

In today's business environment we are competing as fiercely to attract and retain talented people as we are to win clients. Lack of resource is a widespread problem. We need

to provide an environment in which people thrive, where they want to stay, and where they can achieve their full potential – for themselves and for KPMG. This is not always a comfortable environment. It is one where people will be stretched – but they will also be respected, supported, coached and given limitless opportunities.

The environment we need is one which provides:

- Respect, **support** and trust
- Varied, challenging and rewarding work and planned career **development**
- **Teamwork**: self-fulfilment through working and growing together.

INDIVIDUALS WILL DEMONSTRATE THIS VALUE BY:

- Treating all colleagues with courtesy, consideration and respect
- Listening to and valuing the opinions of others, even when they do not agree with them
- Helping others in the firm to succeed
- Communicating openly and honestly
- Seeking out, listening to and responding to feedback
- Conscientiously adopting the role of mentoring, counselling and developing others
- Considering staff development needs when allocating work
- Investing time and funds in retaining and developing people
- Actively encouraging teamwork
- Taking into consideration quality-of-life issues
- Rewarding and recognising people appropriately
- Helping people learn from mistakes
- Giving each person ample opportunities to develop professionally, even if it means losing that person to another team
- Meeting commitments to others.

KPMG WILL NOT TOLERATE INDIVIDUALS WHO UNDERMINE THIS VALUE BY:

- Blaming and criticising others
- Neglecting mentoring, counselling or other development activities
- Failing to give feedback
- Automatically putting client interests before staff interests at all times
- Giving a low priority to one's own and others' learning and development
- Expecting people to work unreasonably long hours
- Favouring certain people and being unfairly prejudiced against others
- Taking unjustified credit for success
- Promoting one's self at the expense of others
- Being reluctant to give new people a chance
- Discouraging people from development activities such as training and secondments
- Basing performance evaluation only on revenues brought in, and not on people skills.

WE WILL KNOW THAT WE ARE PRACTISING THIS VALUE WHEN:

- Our ability to attract and retain talented people improves significantly, and outstrips that of our competitors
- We rank highly in ratings of preferred employers
- Our clients compliment us on the calibre of our people
- Our present employees and partners enjoy being here, while KPMG alumni retain good relationships with us.

'WE CONTINUOUSLY EXTEND THE FRONTIERS OF OUR SHARED **KNOWLEDGE**'

KPMG has a tremendous wealth of intellect, experience and ideas. To turn this knowledge into value, we need to

preserve, share, expand, and apply our knowledge effectively. New systems and processes will help us do this – but tools and techniques are not enough. We also need the mindset, motivation and will to use them.

This means:

- **Openness** of mind and continuous learning
- Treating knowledge as a highly valued **asset**
- Ensuring everyone in the firm has a right and an **obligation** to access our knowledge base, and the responsibility to contribute to it.

INDIVIDUALS WILL DEMONSTRATE THIS VALUE BY:

- Promoting formal and informal learning for themselves and others
- Being curious about and open to new ideas
- Devoting time to sharing their own knowledge with others
- Turning informal knowledge into processes and services that benefit the firm
- Informing themselves of what knowledge, processes and methodologies exist in KPMG, and encouraging their use
- Investing in the development and use of worldwide knowledge-sharing systems
- Reflecting on and learning from successes and failures, and sharing this with others
- Taking time out to debrief teams, in order to capture and communicate learning
- Seeking out and learning from specialists within and outside the firm
- Charging for the quality of knowledge and the amount of value brought to the client, rather than just for hours spent.

KPMG WILL NOT TOLERATE INDIVIDUALS WHO UNDERMINE THIS VALUE BY:

- Hoarding knowledge and information
- Ignoring knowledge and methodologies which were 'not invented here'
- Persisting in doing things differently despite the existence of KPMG processes
- Neglecting the personal development needs of one's self and others
- Failing to keep up-to-date on current thinking in the profession or the market
- Using knowledge as a source of personal power
- Always insisting upon being right, or claiming to have all the answers
- Focusing on weaknesses in others' ideas or knowledge
- Allowing useful knowledge to go unnoticed or be lost
- Being reluctant to spend time or resources in gathering and recording learning.

WE WILL KNOW THAT WE ARE PRACTISING THIS VALUE WHEN:

- Our profits improve – because we have ceased to duplicate effort in developing our knowledge, and because we can charge a premium for the value that our knowledge adds to the client
- We are recognised as being at the leading edge of our professions, and ahead of our competitors
- Our staff retention improves because people value the knowledge and learning they can acquire at KPMG.

The Secret Weapon: The Global Values Game
Around the beginning of 1999, people at KPMG were beginning to suspect that I had finally gone too far. I had been spotted on more than one occasion in meeting rooms with a selection of victims, huddled around a brightly coloured circular board. Laughter and the sound of rolling dice could be heard in the

corridors. Cards were shuffled, deals were cut and there was the occasional groan or heated exchange. And, more bizarre than that, when discovered in such situations, I claimed that I was working. Some people worried that Colin didn't know what his team got up to half the time. Others worried that he did.

When I had had the vision of the toolkit packaged as a little doctor's case, I had at the same time hit on the idea of a board game. As it turned out, the doctor's case was just a passing fancy, but I was completely in love with the idea of the board game. Which was just as well, because only true love and commitment stopped me from throwing it out the window on more than one occasion.

Developing a board game is a frustrating experience. Just when you think you have got it nearly right, you change the slightest little detail and the whole dynamics of the game get thrown into chaos. I worked with my friend David on the development of the game. Although now a consultant, David is a philosopher by education while I used to be a theoretical physicist. You would think, given this, that we would have been able to calculate everything nicely and produce the thing in near perfect form. But no. In the end you just have to try a lot of stuff out, fiddle around and test it on live animals. During the trials of the many prototypes, I would often find myself sitting in a room with the game set up, waiting for my guinea-pigs to arrive (sometimes having bribed them with food and drink), under the curious scrutiny of passers-by.

The justification for the board game was that the values implementation process needed something unconventional – something which would inject life into it. We were at that critical point in a long-term internal project where people easily lose interest. The toolkit provided many innovative techniques for carrying out culture change, but we needed to go one step further in capturing the imagination of people in the firm if we were to keep up the momentum. We also felt that although everyone had received oral and written communications about the new culture, the values would only come to life if people actually tested and experienced them. People in KPMG still needed to learn about the values, but we did not want to lecture them or bore them to death in the process. Hence the secret weapon: the *Global Values Game*.

We decided that the game should model KPMG as an organisation and that people would actually have to play according to KPMG's values to win it. (Nice idea, but how on earth were we to put it into practice?) In the end we drew our inspiration from the game of 'Monopoly', except that instead of playing with properties, houses and hotels we played the game with clients, people and knowledge (there are our three assets, making an appearance yet again). The board is divided up into three geographic regions, just as KPMG is in real life. Key clients from each region are displayed around the edge of the board, and the three players (one from each region), use their resources, that is, their people and knowledge, to win client relationships and do engagements, thus earning money. In simple terms, that's exactly what KPMG does in real life. Squares were added to the board which forced players to think about developing their people and investing in their knowledge base, and wild cards were added with questions about the values, as well as the obligatory 'chance' and 'community' cards.

The real triumph of the game is that it picks up on the one behaviour which it is most important that KPMG gets right: team-work. Players quickly find that they can only serve their clients best, and win the highest-value engagements, if they share resources – people and knowledge – with their colleagues in other geographic regions. The game is set up so that, if players learn to trust each other, to share resources and rewards, and to co-operate globally, everyone benefits. Just as in real life, the KPMG regions are not playing against each other, but are in fact trying to best serve their clients and raise the value of the firm globally. The game is designed to be played in large groups with more than one board set up at once. Games run in parallel so that at the end of the session the total scores for each board can be compared. Players who realise that they are not in fact competing against the people around their own board, but are competing against the other boards in the room, end up with very high scores. At the beginning of the game, people are told that it is just like KPMG in real life. In real life, KPMG people know that our three geographic regions are not acting only in their own interests, but that they are all working together to compete against PwC, Ernst & Young, Andersens and so on.

All the trials of the prototypes paid off: we finally reached a point where the game seemed to run without any hitches. It was just as well, because I was quickly running out of people to test it on. (Staff at KPMG's head office in London were finding it more and more difficult to excuse themselves from other commitments by saying 'I'm sorry, I have to go and play a game now'.) The design company turned the game into a thing of beauty and suddenly it was ready to be launched on the unsuspecting KPMG population. Aptly, the very first group to play the game was KPMG's International Council. The session was conducted over lunch at their meeting in Melbourne in April 1999 – almost two years after that initial meeting in Dublin where we had talked about values for the first time. It was like a baptism of fire, since prior to the meeting I had only been able to test the final version of the game once on a small group with only two boards in play. Now here I was in a conference room in Australia with about forty of KPMG's most senior people peeping in the door and wondering what was going on. Six tables had been set up with the game, and the Council were divided up into groups of six or seven to play it. As it turned out, the session ran very smoothly. The game worked well and they had great fun playing it. One group achieved a very high score and were pronounced the winners. They were very smug. Everyone seemed to get a lot out of it. However, one very senior person did catch up with me for a chat later that afternoon.

> 'Great game, Jan, great. You should have told us at the start though, that we weren't competing against each other, but that we were trying to beat the other boards . . .'
>
> 'But I did tell you.'
>
> 'No you didn't!' (Oops! Remember the values!) 'I mean, . . . ah . . . I don't recall that you did . . .'
>
> 'I did tell you. Well – not directly I suppose, but I did tell you it was just like real life in KPMG.'
>
> 'Ah ha ha ha ha ha. Very funny. Ha ha ha. Yes of course in *real life*, I would have behaved completely differently. But . . . uh

. . . I . . . uh . . . yes well, very clever, very clever indeed! Well done!'

The game did the rounds of various conferences and development programmes after that. It always worked well, especially in large groups. So far, the group which did best was, ironically (or come to think of it, maybe not that ironic) the most junior – about eighty managers from all over KPMG's European region. They seemed to catch on to the fact that they should share resources and not argue too much about how to divide up rewards sooner than their more senior colleagues. That gave us hope for the future!

In summary, the game was a means of livening up the implementation process and making communication fun. It also helped people to learn about the values by putting them into practice. Children learn through play, so there is no reason why adults should always have to wade through corporate literature or sit through presentations to do the same.

The game was indeed a secret weapon. It drew an enormous amount of interest. At one point I was concerned that the game was being talked about so much that everyone would forget its more serious sister, the toolkit, but fortunately this did not happen. On the contrary, the game was effective in marketing the idea of the toolkit and culture change in general. It has given the implementation effort a surge of momentum and enthusiasm.

I do not propose that everyone about to embark on culture change develops a board game, but I do believe that every culture change benefits from *some* unconventional approaches. Something slightly different, which is wacky enough to capture people's attention while still being grounded enough to bear a worthwhile message, will keep the interest in a long-term project alive.

Conclusion
In our experience at KPMG, we found that the benefit of the toolkit approach was in maintaining flexibility, offering people choices about what to do whether they were engaged in a full-scale culture change programme or whether they were just running a few simple initiatives. It was also important to show people something

tangible which could be used in a very practical way to bring about culture change. This helped dispel the all-too-common myth that culture change is a fluffy, nebulous thing.

Culture change presents almost limitless scope for activities, so no toolkit can ever be complete. This chapter has described the basics of KPMG's approach. These are a good starting point for developing a culture change programme, but the most important ingredients – imagination, drive and understanding of the unique characteristics of the organisation – need to be supplied by the change agent.

Chapter 5

FACILITATING THE PROCESS

We have talked enough now about tools and techniques for culture change. We can now pause from examining nuts and bolts to consider a few deeper questions – what is a culture change programme like this likely to achieve? What does it feel like to facilitate a process like this and what lessons can be learned from the experiences gained at KPMG?

At KPMG we are almost three years into our culture change programme. An enormous amount of ground has been covered and it is a good time to reflect on what we have achieved. This chapter captures those reflections, including a review of how far KPMG has progressed in its culture change efforts as well as some of my own experiences of facilitating the process, including some of the lessons learned about the more gritty aspects of running a culture change initiative.

Where KPMG is at
'How will we know when we have got there?'

We asked KPMG people all over the world to answer this question when we painted a picture of our desired culture. Some of the answers appear in the document entitled 'Practising our Values' which was reproduced in the last chapter – you might remember statements about how we will be ahead of our competitors in winning and retaining clients, attracting talented people, utilising and sharing our knowledge. How our people will feel that they are really adding superior value to clients, how proficient a place it will be to work. How our client relationships, profits and revenues will improve. All these will tell us we have achieved our goals for the culture change.

Have we got there? Of course not. Any process of culture change will be lengthy, and KPMG's is no exception. The firm is still in the early days of implementation. However, in the two and a half years of the project to date, we have at least established ourselves firmly on the path to 'getting there' – let's take a look at what has been achieved:

We have achieved perhaps the most important step of all on the path to culture change: we have changed how people at KPMG think. There is a deeper understanding of the importance of the firm's culture, a high level of awareness of our values and a firm grasp of how they should be put into practice. These attitudes simply did not exist before. The values are well and truly *there*. They are called upon for guidance in day-to-day situations. People might not always act according to the values, but they know they *should* be acting according to the values. They know that in the future, values will no longer feature on the list of things you can 'get away with not doing'. Behavioural change, unheard of a few years ago, is now a focus of attention and actions are being undertaken throughout the firm to ensure that it happens.

There is a strong sense that the values are shared by all. There is buy-in to the values statement – and the behaviours which support it – all over the world. Our efforts to involve people from throughout the global firm paid off. Perhaps this is why the interest and enthusiasm for the values process remains strong, and there is still commitment to implementation even after Colin's retirement from the international chairmanship. The values banner is still being held high by KPMG's international leaders. Steve Butler, KPMG's present International Chairman, continues to sponsor culture change at a global level. Other key international leaders have also become crusaders for the values and have achieved astonishing results in their practices and regions.

As a result of strong sponsorship, there has been a good take-up of the values implementation toolkit (and the game, needless to say), with many practices either using it in developing their own culture change programmes or integrating the tools into their existing activities. People have responded well to the toolkit because it provides rigorous techniques but is also flexible and easy to use.

The values have been integrated into our existing organisational programmes both internationally and locally. At the highest level, we see the values manifested in our strategic decision-making. Decisions about investment, for example into knowledge management, global client account management and the development of HR strategy and policies, have all been influenced by the values. On a day-to-day basis, the values are being built into our business processes, our reward and recognition systems and other 'artefacts' of our culture. The connection between values and reality has been made.

In summary, we might not have reached the stage where we can honestly say 'because of our culture change, our staff retention is better' or 'our profits have improved'. But let's face it, these are very long-term aspirations. In the meantime, we are busy 'learning' the new culture. KPMG is starting to feel different and we are seeing the direct application of the values in our decisions and actions. There is still much enthusiasm and momentum for implementation. In all, we can be content with the progress we have made so far.

Of course it has not all been a bed of roses. There have been problems along the way and there are still problems now. Putting positive achievements aside, let's have a look at some of the issues:

One problem which has not gone away is that KPMG is just so *big*. Particularly in the implementation phase, when the process is no longer being run centrally, it is hard to maintain an overview and give appropriate support. There is still much work to be done before everyone in KPMG, irrespective of location, truly understands and acts according to the values. Coping with the sheer size of an organisation which until recently had been very fragmented has been difficult, but fortunately the firm's recent restructuring and ongoing globalisation programme is making things easier. The firm is still big (which is good of course!), but no longer fragmented, so while the scale of the programme is still massive, at least the problems which arose due to inconsistencies and various other fallings-out have diminished.

Resourcing the implementation also presents difficulties. Not every KPMG practice is able to find appropriately skilled change agents to design and run their culture initiatives. Some practices have resolved this by sharing resources with their neighbours, while others look to larger practices or their regional head offices for support. In the end, we are content if each of our national practices moves as fast as it can given the existing constraints, accepting that some can move very fast and achieve a great deal, while others may take more time to catch up.

Another issue is that although there is a strong business case for culture change, it is not felt with equal acuteness in all KPMG's national practices. We still have some practices which flourish in their local markets without having to pay attention to the values. For example, while the competition for talented staff is fierce in most Western countries, this is not true all over the world. It is hard to convince a senior partner that without culture change, staff retention will become a real problem, when there is a legion of bright graduates beating down his door asking for jobs. As part of the firm's longer-term strategy development, we have invested considerable effort in looking at trends and future scenarios. We are convinced that if we neglect any of our values, our business will be unsustainable in the longer term, but it remains a fact that immediate threats provide more motivation than distant ones when it comes to putting the effort into change. The lesson to learn from this is that the business case needs to be more than strong: it also needs to impart a real sense of urgency. In the pockets of KPMG where the sense of urgency regarding culture change is lacking, we need to reach out further to find more far-sighted advocates and sponsors of change.

The maintenance of consistency throughout the process was a nightmare which only recently appears to have ended. There were some good reasons for why consistency was a problem. For example, many practices had already developed their own sets of values *before* the international culture change programme started. A few had gone even further and begun to implement significant culture change. Although any work on values done by KPMG's national practices around the world was acknowledged and used as input to the international process, it was nonetheless understandable that such practices were unwilling to abandon their 'own' values in favour of the global statement. In other words, at times we had several competing values statements out there. While this was frustrating, we needed to appreciate the perspective of local leaders. They could hardly turn around to their people and say 'These values you have all been working towards are now out! And as of tomorrow, these new international ones are in!' For such practices, the transition to the adoption of the international values needed to be a managed process. Fortunately, this has followed as a natural consequence of KPMG's globalisation effort.

There were also some less acceptable reasons for why consistency was a problem, the main one being that KPMG's old habit of reinventing the wheel dies hard in some parts of the firm. In one or two of our national practices, we found that people were re-formulating the values statement in their own words or changing bits and pieces of it. Generally, their sentiments were identical to those of the global values statement, but the fact that the words were different made it hard to maintain clarity. We also saw some national practices from time to time engaging in activities which had already been covered by the international process. It felt a little like they were running on the spot – repeating what had already been done rather than moving forward. However, we had to accept that in the area of culture change sometimes people do have to revisit or repeat activities to make things 'stick'. In dealing with people's beliefs and behaviours, it sometimes isn't enough to say 'Here's one we prepared earlier'. At times the process looked messy, but we had to avoid getting too precious about it. In the end, clarity of the message was maintained through sheer persistence and we have managed to achieve consistency in the vast majority of our practices. We are content with that for now.

There is another issue for which the jury might still be out. How consequent will KPMG really be in penalising people who do not comply with the values? In the past, it was impossible to 'get tough' on practices which did not comply with international policy because of the nature of KPMG's structure and governance. That difficulty has now been removed through the implementation of a new structure and membership agreement for the global firm. The distribution of authority is now such that policies are easier to enforce. However, rules and regulations aside, people in KPMG also suffer from a rare condition known as 'terminal niceness', which manifests itself in a general unwillingness to challenge or penalise bad behaviour. In the past, we have often been far too tolerant. Now new voices are emerging which are more forceful and focused. Leaders of the firm internationally are saying that they will no longer tolerate people who undermine the values, even if they are star performers in terms of revenue generation. People are getting to the stage where they think that leadership is in fact serious about this, especially since they have seen evidence of it, for example in the introduction of 360° feedback in appraisal and development processes. This 'getting tough' thing is a big step for KPMG, and it is all part of learning the new culture.

Culture change is a struggle lasting many years, and it requires constant energy and revitalisation to keep it moving forward. While I was pleased to get the culture change off the ground, others at KPMG later joined in as champions of the process, adding their own style, flair and creativity. With Steve Butler of the USA as KPMG's International Chairman, the global effort has shifted up a gear, moving even more quickly and increasing the focus on individual commitment to the new values.

The process of learning the new culture sometimes feels like it's 'one step forward, two steps back'. At KPMG there have been cases when the practice of a new value or behaviour has been visibly upheld ten times over, but the positive effects of this have been instantly negated by a thoughtless word or action reminiscent of the old culture. Of course we have tried to avoid slipping up as much as possible, but inevitably, errors have occurred. In such cases we just had to be prepared to start all over again. Persistence was key. So it is with culture change. With continual reinforcement of the desired culture and an open acknowledgement of mistakes when throwbacks from the old culture rear their ugly heads, these setbacks can eventually be overcome.

Sometimes people worry that we have not resolved the inherent dilemmas in our culture. The values are supposed to guide us in our actions and decision-making. They should enable us to make wise choices. But sometimes the values themselves give rise to dilemmas. I was asked once how for example, we can always ensure that we offer clients the best possible service while at the same time ensuring that our staff can maintain a balance of life? The answer is: I don't know. It all comes down to the discretion applied to decisions made on each individual case. We can't make a rule about it. But to me, the fact that this question is being asked is a sign that culture change is happening. In the past, this dilemma would not even have arisen in KPMG – the client need would have won every time. Now because managers in the firm are familiar with the values, they have to consider various options in situations like these. A new culture does not make dilemmas go away. It just gives us better quality dilemmas to reconcile.

In summary, we are happy with the progress we have made in changing KPMG's culture, but there is still much to be done. Cultural and behavioural change is slow. It requires patience and persistence. We are learning all the time. We feel we are well on the way to achieving our goals but we are under no illusions that there will be no further problems. There is, however, no doubt that things are different now from three years ago. In an organisation where the largest single group consists of male accountants, culture, values and behaviour are talked about freely. Surely that is a measure of success!

What the textbooks don't tell you about facilitating culture change

We have lived with KPMG's culture change process for two and a half years and have learned a great deal. We have also advised on and found out what other organisations struggle with in changing their culture. The final chapter of this book combines our experience with general wisdom, theory and best practice to look at the wider implications of culture, and gives advice to anyone undertaking culture change in an organisation, irrespective of its size or type.

However, there are also a few lessons gained from my personal experience as the change agent facilitating KPMG's process which are worth sharing with you here. Looking back over the past three years, there are six things which I wish someone had told me at the very start:

Lesson No. 1: Make it intelligent, but don't be afraid to state the obvious

Lesson No. 2: Appreciate the whole picture

Lesson No. 3: You are not a magician or a police officer

Lesson No. 4: Shoot anyone who says that culture is the responsibility of the HR function

Lesson No. 5: Know when to let go

Lesson No. 6: At the end of the day, you will have to do it yourselves

Lesson No. 1: Make it intelligent, but don't be afraid to state the obvious

People are not born with a natural understanding of organisational culture. It needs to be explained to them. In our work with groups in KPMG we took a lot of time to explain the background to our thinking, and what we were asking people to do. This raised the quality of discussion and made for a better working atmosphere.

Most people like to learn and will appreciate it if you take some time to explain. To show that you respect this, explanations have to be intelligent, that is, well thought through and rigorous. (Bear in mind the old adage that if you can't explain something, then you don't understand it yourself.) However, 'intelligent' does not mean 'lacking in simplicity'. Quite the opposite. A key to understanding is saying what you mean in everyday language.

Nor does 'intelligent' mean that you will not have to state the obvious. I had always thought that stating the obvious to someone was patronising, and a waste of time. Then one day I was having a discussion with an HR professional in KPMG. We were discussing how to bring the values into the appraisal system, and he said that people were unclear about what sort of behaviours supported the values. 'But that's obvious!' I protested. Obvious to me, perhaps, and probably obvious to anyone who had ten minutes to spare to think about it. But it is so much easier not to have to spend that ten minutes thinking about it. Stating the obvious can save people time, reinforce the message and contribute to making things absolutely clear. And – let's be cynical for a moment – if you state the obvious, there can be no excuses for misunderstanding.

If you will excuse me for stating the obvious for a second: there is, of course, a balance to be maintained between assuming someone's intelligence about a matter and stating the obvious. Achieving the right balance requires sensitivity and an understanding of the audience. When all is said and done, however, no one will be upset if you communicate with clarity.

Lesson No. 2: Appreciate the whole picture
Culture permeates every element of the organisation, so if you are managing culture change you have to appreciate the full picture.

You have to understand the organisation's past: its origins, major influences and events, its histories of successes and failures, the patterns that keep repeating themselves. In this way you can be aware of what obstacles and opportunities are likely to occur in the future.

You have to understand fully the present organisation. This means familiarising yourself with the day-to-day working of the organisation, making links and building relationships. You have to appreciate the effect of your activities on other areas, and how their activities will affect what you are doing.

Culture change is all about bringing the organisation's vision into being, so you need to understand where the company is going. You need to understand the role of culture in the company's future, and ensure that the strategic goals reflect the vision and values.

Gaining an appreciation of the full picture is perhaps one of the most rewarding aspects of this kind of work. To see a whole system in operation, understand why it is the way it is and to help the organisation move to its desired future is a privilege which more than makes up for the flak and frustration sustained along the way.

Lesson No. 3: You are not a magician or a police officer
I used to work in a small team with two other women. After a while we found out that people had been referring to us as 'the three witches'. With the Spanish Inquisition safely behind us, we reckoned that there were worse things that people could be saying about us. I assumed that it was that sort of teasingly affectionate nickname you get in KPMG. Then one day I realised that some people did in fact think that I had magical powers. And culture change was the magic. Cultural and behavioural change, pooh-poohed in KPMG for so long, suddenly became the thing that would save us. As long as we had 'teamwork', everything would miraculously be alright! And – as a change agent, all you needed to do was cast one of your little spells and everyone would undergo a complete personality transformation in eight months. People can sometimes get carried away with culture change. Yes, it is very important. Yes, it can help to dramatically improve the performance of an organisation. No, it can't solve *all* the organisation's problems. And no, there is no magic formula to make it happen overnight. The formula is no secret – it's just hard work and a lot of time.

When the miracle didn't happen, it didn't take long to convince people that I was not a magician. I emerged from witchery fresh and ready to assume my next persona: Head of the Values Police. The values police are appointed to enforce the values law. For example, the values police will sometimes be asked to attend a meeting to make sure that everyone is acting according to the values. They are asked to intervene if the values are being infringed. This is handy, because it saves everyone else from taking any responsibility to make sure that the values law is not broken. Unfortunately, the notion doesn't work, because no one wants to live in a police state. Most societies function because the majority of citizens consciously try not to break the law. They take responsibility for their own behaviour. This responsibility can't be delegated to others. When facilitating culture change, you can help raise people's awareness of the values law, but don't get yourself into a situation where you are the only person taking the responsibility to enforce it.

I have exaggerated somewhat here, but I do want to make a point that the change agent needs to be clear about what his or her responsibilities are and also *where they end*. Other people's expectations about the role also need to be carefully managed. Otherwise it is all too easy for change agents to take on things for which they are not responsible or which they have no authority to resolve. I remember one incident which brought this home to me: I was on my way to the airport at the end of a business trip and was carrying a small but very heavy backpack. I was spotted en route by KPMG's International CEO, Paul Reilly. He quipped, 'Have you got the values in there, Jan?' At the time, I did feel like I was carrying them around like a burden on my back. It was a joke, but a good reality check all the same.

Lesson No. 4: Shoot anyone who says that culture is the responsibility of the HR function

There is a word-association game which is played at lightning speed in organisations when it comes to deciding who will bear the brunt of the culture change effort. It goes like this and takes about ten nanoseconds to play:

'Uhhh . . . Culture – that's a people issue – people – HR. Yes, HR will do it.'

And before anyone can say 'Whoa – hang on a minute', everyone has left the room, abandoning the crestfallen HR professional with a list of impossible tasks.

Of course the HR function has a very significant role to play in culture change. But so do all the other support functions. Culture change needs to touch *every* element of the organisation, not just HR processes.

Culture and culture change are primarily the responsibility of *leadership*. Dumping the sole responsibility on the HR function is an evasion. It's *wrong*. Still, almost every client organisation I have worked with, and many KPMG member firms, have at some point fallen into this all too convenient trap. As a change agent, you need to constantly be aware of this tendency, to educate people at every opportunity and to challenge it every time it arises.

As key sponsor of KPMG's culture change, there were four main lessons I learned from my involvement, which I believe would be of use to anyone in a leadership position. First, unless the Chief Executive or Chairman is prepared to spend a lot of time on this over a long period, it's not worth bothering at all – without that commitment at the top, the process will fail. Secondly, involve as many people in the organisation as possible in an open and frank discussion of where you are now and where you need to be. Thirdly, the new shared values should be expressed generically for the whole organisation, but behavioural interpretations of the values should be allowed to differ from place to place. Lastly, it is ultimately the job of everyone in management to make the change happen; every manager must live the new culture, champion it at every opportunity, and integrate it at every level with the way the organisation works. When all is said and done, culture change is simply about bringing diverse people together, getting them to buy into a shared ideal, and working very hard to bring that ideal to life.

Lesson No. 5: Know when to let go

I once attended a major event run by one of our member firms at which the audience spent a lot of time working on values and behaviour. I was a guest and had had virtually no input into the event. The session was running superbly well. The participants were excited by the process and very engaged. I was feeling . . . encouraged? No. Energised? No. Happy? No. I was feeling grumpy.

I was feeling grumpy because the event wasn't being run *quite* like I would have done it. Every now and again I'd think 'Oh, they missed an opportunity there. They should have done this. They should have done that. Why did he have to say it that way and not this way?' Fortunately the Thought Police were not around. Otherwise I would have been arrested on charges of First Degree Control Freakery. As it turned out, the event was a huge success – no doubt because there were good reasons not to do things the way I would have done them.

It is hard, when you have poured your energy and enthusiasm

into something, to let go. But change agents who do not know when to let go end up doing more harm than good. One person cannot do everything – nor should they. There comes a point when processes need to evolve in their own way, and be led by other people. I'm not a parent myself, but I imagine it is similar to how you might feel when your children leave home. You know it would be bad for your children and for you if you were still looking after them throughout adulthood, but you feel sad to see them go all the same.

Lesson No. 6: At the end of the day, you will have to do it yourselves

Culture is unique for every organisation. The values in the culture reflect what is authentically believed by the people in the organisation. They have intrinsic worth. They describe what the organisation stands for, and are something which people in the organisation will hold dear through generations.

Given this, it is not difficult to see that culture needs to be understood and worked on from *within* the organisation. No external adviser will understand your culture as well as you do, or will be able to think up a set of values for you. External advisers might be able to help you with the *process* you might follow, but they will not be able to do the work *for* you. How could they? Values are about the beliefs of the people inside the organisation, so who better to do it than yourselves?

Another thing which I find incredible is the way some people think they can 'borrow' values from other organisations. They take a fancy to some successful organisation's values statement and say, 'Why don't we just use that?' They neglect to think about the beliefs and characteristics of their *own* organisation. Remember we drew parallels between company cultures and individual personalities? Can you imagine saying – 'I'm going out tonight, so I'll just adopt Billy Connolly's personality and liven up the party a bit'? Of course not. You have no choice but to go to the party with your own personality. In the same way, organisations have no choice but to go to market as themselves. No one wants an imitation.

The Seventh Lesson: A Treatise on Management Consultants

There is a seventh lesson to be learned which does not fit neatly into the above scheme. This lesson applies not only to change agents, but also to the many consultants whom change agents might, in the course of their endeavours, have the pleasure or the regret of encountering.

As a client, you might often benefit from hiring in someone from outside. You will discover that, particularly when it comes to culture change, there is an overwhelming number of (mostly small) consultancies vying to assist you. You just need to find the right ones. As a consultant, you know that it is in your and the client's best interests to build a lasting business relationship. So why is it, that with two willing parties who both want the same thing, the path of the consulting relationship does not always run smooth? Why is it that consultants and clients who are both genuinely committed to a successful outcome, suddenly find themselves in a mess of miscommunication, misunderstanding and disappointed expectations?

I have experienced the consulting relationship from both sides. Prior to taking up my role in leading KPMG's culture change effort, I myself worked as a management consultant to other organisations. In the past three years, the boot has been on the other foot: I have experienced life as a client. I have been responsible for hiring and working with a wide range of consultants. This has been what a management consultant might call 'a unique learning opportunity'. A normal human being might say 'an eye-opener'. In other words, while I have worked with some great people, I have also found out what consultants do wrong as well as what they do right in managing their client relationships.

The following section is a bit of a digression from the main theme of this book – but justified, I think. Because I really do feel that the business world would be a better place if clients and consultants understood one another a little better.

Eight Golden Rules for Management Consultants

Let me first tell you the story of the £350K £40K proposal. While developing the values toolkit, I felt I needed some help in coping with the sheer volume of work, particularly when it came to putting together the communications tools. My colleagues at KPMG were working flat out and unable to spare enough time for what was needed, so I decided to seek help from external consultants. I developed a very specific brief and asked a few small consultancies to come in and bid for the work. I am a co-operative client and wanted to make things as easy as possible. Prior to the proposal process, I invited both candidates in for a lengthy briefing session. I gave them the brief, some background and, I hoped, a better feel for what was needed. To give them an idea of the scope of the work, I told them that I imagined that it would command a fee of £40-£50K. Not much by McKinsey standards I admit, but it was a foot in the door with a blue-chip client.

A few weeks later, I met with both consultancies to go through their proposals. One company sent one of their senior staff out to talk me through a simple, written document. Their proposal restated much of what I had said in the brief, outlined clearly what they would do and gave an estimated fee of about £40-£50K. So far, so good. The other consultancy appeared with three representatives and a huge pack of PowerPoint slides. They were bursting with ideas which went far beyond the mundane task of developing a few tools and techniques for a toolkit. For example, they proposed to set up a 'war room' near my office (staffed permanently by about three of their people), to design and run a lengthy retreat for KPMG's International Board, to develop multi-media communications for KPMG worldwide and to manage the implementation of KPMG's values throughout the global firm (hang on – wasn't that *my* job?). All this wonderful stuff we didn't need for (printed on the last page of the mammoth proposal . . .) a sum of £350-£380K.

I am not a particularly decisive person, but it didn't take long for me to make up my mind. When the £350K people rang up to ask why they had not been chosen, I told them that I had not found in their proposal what I had asked them to do. They were enthusiastic, which was good. They had plenty of ideas, which was also good. But they had not *listened* (which was a bit ironic, given that they were communications consultants).

So if I were to write the golden rules of consulting, I would begin as follows:

Rule No. 1: Listen to your client
If you go into a fruit shop asking for bananas, you will be pretty annoyed if the assistant gives you a sack of oranges instead. Your client is no different. *Listen* to what they are asking you to do.

When I added up the time spent preparing the brief, sitting in meetings and searching through the gargantuan, mind-popping proposal document for something that resembled what I had asked these people to do, it came to quite a chunky part of my week. I know that the £350K £40K team had put a lot of time and energy into the proposal and I know they were disappointed not to get the work. They may have regretted the time they wasted. I wonder did they ever stop to think about the time *I* wasted? Clients will inevitably have to invest a lot of time looking at proposals which they end up rejecting. This is all a necessary part of the selection process. But you know, clients don't actually *enjoy* doing this, and they might just have one or two other, more pressing things to do. Which is all the more reason to abide by the following rule:

Rule No. 2: Your client's time is precious – don't waste it
Don't just think about your time input into a proposal or project – think about the consequences for the client's time too. You don't want to waste your own time, so don't waste theirs either. Make things easy for them.

Let's move off the subject of the £350K £40K proposal and I will introduce you to The Glums. The Glums (not their real names) are a small consultancy specialising in business psychology. I met them early on in the values process – I think quite some time prior to the development of the toolkit. I was excited when I met them because they appeared to offer something which many consultancies in this field do not. They seemed quite academic, but also very experienced and rigorous. You might say 'heavyweight'. They didn't seem like the kind of people who would offer standard solutions or propose communal foot washes as a means of team bonding. I thought they could perhaps help us quite significantly, and we had several lengthy meetings to work out what we might do together.

The thing about The Glums was that they were just so . . . well . . . so damn *glum*. They always appeared to have had a row with each other before they came to see us. You could often sense a tension between them. And they weren't too friendly with us either. They grumbled about stuff. They were cold, reserved, miserable and even arrogant at times. As mentioned already, in KPMG it is terribly important to be nice. It is a main attraction of the firm that it employs personable, friendly and warm people. We could not have worked with The Glums, as we ended up calling them, because for all their talents, we just did not like them. Which brings us to the next golden rule of management consultancy:

Rule No. 3: Nobody wants to work with a misery guts
There is enough misery in organisations today without hiring consultants in addition. Only masochists pay people to make them feel bad. Besides, people work better and achieve so much more if they are in good spirits. Relationships are the most important thing in the consulting business. You might be a consultant with a brilliant mind, but you'll only do well if you have a personality to match.

On one occasion, The Glums brought along one of their associates, a stuck-up woman. I can't remember her name, so let's call her Miss Awfully-Awfully. About half an hour into the meeting, Miss Awfully-Awfully had not said a word except to introduce herself. The Glums had obviously had their usual pre-meeting tiff, so they weren't speaking much either. No one was saying much except me. I was trying to explain very frankly the issues, the complexities of the job, what needed to be done and the constraints we were experiencing. I have said before that real change processes look messy and this was no exception. Suddenly Miss Awfully-Awfully interjected with a helpful comment: 'Maybe you need to work out what your job is!' she sneered. 'Maybe you need to **** off' is what I was about to say, but like everyone else in KPMG, I suffer from terminal niceness, so instead I said 'Pardon?'. However, in that moment I decided I would never, ever see that woman again. So what have we learned from this?

Rule No. 4: Nobody wants to work with a smart-arse either

Don't insult your clients, especially at your first meeting. There is a big difference between constructive challenge and downright impudence. For example, clients like the former but not the latter. They want their consultants to be clever, but not arrogant. Show some respect. If you are struggling with this concept, just remember that the client is the one with the cheque book and you are the one asking for work.

The problem with some management consultants is that they think the client expects them to know everything. Well – here's some good news – we don't. We expect you to know all about *your* stuff. But we don't expect you to know about *our* stuff. We know about *our* stuff already, so we would be wasting our money if we asked you to tell us about it. Let me illustrate this with a real-life example. We were working with a young man from a PR agency on the production of a major event. We were discussing how the session on values would be staged at that event. Suddenly we found ourselves in a discussion about the nature of organisational culture. This went off at a tangent, but I didn't mind explaining the background to what we were doing. That is, I didn't mind until he began to present, at great length, his own half-baked theories about how we should be handling culture change – a subject he clearly knew nothing about. Which brings us to Rule No. 5:

Rule No. 5: If you can't resist the urge to bullshit, do it on a subject your client knows nothing about

Of course it would be better not to bullshit at all, but old habits sometimes die hard. If you feel the urge to bullshit coming on, check beforehand that your client knows nothing about the subject. Under no circumstances indulge in bullshitting about a subject in which your client is an expert. You will be found out, the client will get bored and, if you are unlucky, subsequently poke fun at you in a book.

A more common misdemeanour we experienced was that many consultants didn't make us feel as if we were getting their undivided attention. Now, we are all grown up at KPMG. We don't really expect undivided attention. In truth, we would worry if the advisers we hire were not also busy with other clients. We want to work with good people and we know that such people are in demand. However, many of the people who have worked for us have been more than just busy. They have been visibly overstretched. Symptoms of this are:

- constantly introducing different staff on the engagement
- not answering calls
- missing deadlines
- producing 'patchwork quilts' – scrappy deliverables which have obviously been worked on by an army of different people
- saying things like 'I'm terribly busy. I just have to rush off to another client now. Do you mind if I just take this call – it's about a very important job. I have to leave early today because I have another meeting . . . Ooh, I could do with a holiday!'

Overstretched consultants do not make for happy clients. We worry when we see people trying to do too much, because we know their work suffers. We have evidence to prove this, unfortunately. We know that, particularly in small service organisations, it is difficult to resist taking on too much – but at least spare us the worry and pretend to us that you're coping. It's not up to me to tell people not to overstretch their resources, so I would formulate Rule No. 6 as follows:

Rule No. 6: Don't make it obvious that you are overstretched
Make your client feel as if theirs is your most important account.

Deep down, we know this is not true, but indulge us in this fantasy, would you? And calm down.

I once hired a consultancy which habitually missed deadlines. I didn't really get upset about the missed deadlines, because although I'd like to think otherwise, KPMG won't grind to a standstill if a few of my projects come in a couple of days late. What I did get upset about was the fact that I was never *told* that the deadline was going to be missed. You would think that most consultants would know that miracles rarely happen. For example, if, two days before a deadline, there is still five days' worth of work to do, simple mathematics tells us that they will be three days late. It happens to all of us. But why don't they *say so*? Do they think they might slip into a time-warp and make the deadline after all? I'm not telepathic. If I have been told to expect a deliverable on Tuesday, I do not organise my work schedule on the assumption that it will arrive on Friday. A lot of consultants think that 'communication skills' are only about giving good presentations. Sure, that's part of it. But good communication goes further than that – clients want to be updated every now and again about what's going on and they want to know about any hiccups in advance. A simple, timely phone-call will suffice. Do this and a client will forgive you anything.

While we're on the subject of communication, let's pause to pick again on the poor souls who submitted the £350K £40K proposal. The following incident happened when they were talking me through their proposal document. Somewhere on about page 50 of the PowerPoint monolith, I paused in astonishment.

'What's this?' I asked, pointing to a weird-looking graphic.

'Ah – it's supposed to be a telephone . . .'

'It looks like a toilet.'

'Erm, ha ha, well, I suppose it does a bit – but it's supposed to be a telephone, because we're talking about electronic communications media on that slide . . .'

'Oh.'

We all had a laugh about it – it wasn't disastrous for them. However, when I later showed the proposal to one of my colleagues for comment, he advised me against hiring them without even reading the proposal properly. When I asked him how he had arrived at such a quick conclusion, he said:

'Well, for a communications consultancy, these are pretty cruddy slides.'

What's the message here, apart from 'Don't let anyone on drugs loose with the latest version of ClipArt'? The message is to choose appropriate communications media. Flashy is not always best. You don't have to dazzle people with technology to look professional. You do have to choose media which reflect well on you, which support, rather than distract from what you are trying to say and which you think your client will respond to. With the latter point, remember that your client will have seen a lot of slide-packs – you might consider using a different approach for a change. I imagine that a lot of clients are like me, all slide-packed out.

In the interest of clear communication, let's summarise all this in the next rule:

Rule No. 7: Communicate with your client
Communication doesn't stop outside presentations and meetings – it's also about letting your client know, on a day-to-day basis, what's going on. Pick up the phone. Call your client regularly. And when you do have a more formal communication to make, choose appropriate media and go for clarity.

One of the biggest mistakes which consultants have made is to try to sell us what we really didn't want. Although this seems like a silly thing to do, you would be surprised at how frequently it happens. Let's not dwell on the £350K £40K people as culprits any more – here are a few other examples:

Early on in the process I was looking for external consultants to give us fresh ideas on implementing culture change. But more than that, I wanted them to get involved in delivery. I interviewed several people from small, specialised consulting firms. It became something of a private joke within the KPMG team to predict exactly when in the conversation the consultant would sit back, contemplate for a moment and then say, 'I can probably help you best in this if you use me as a sounding board.' Well, what does *that* mean? How about: 'I haven't a clue about how to go about this, but if you don't mind having all the ideas, I'm happy to come along and listen.' What these candidates overlooked was that I was looking for someone to *do stuff*. I wanted someone who was prepared to get their *hands dirty*. I had had enough *talking* about culture change, I now needed to start *doing it*.' In the end, we hired no one.

Other consultants have tried to sell us their own standard solutions, whether they were applicable or not. Sometimes it is really obvious when they try this, like the time a small consultancy came to see me and their MD started to spout their standard, sheep-dip style process at me before her bottom had even warmed the chair. Her process wouldn't have worked in KPMG in a million years – not that she bothered to find that out. However, sometimes the selling of stuff you don't need is more subtle. Gurus can be particularly sneaky. A few of us went to see a famous management guru once for a day's consultation on KPMG's culture change process. It was a fabulous day – very stimulating. On the flight home, our conversation went something like this:

Jan: 'That was so interesting. Fascinating.'
Jennifer: 'He's very bright, isn't he?'
Daniel: 'We really ought to get him involved.'
Jan: 'Yeah.'
Daniel: 'That questionnaire he is developing might be good for . . . um . . . well, I'm sure there's potential to use it somewhere in the firm.'
Jennifer: 'Yes, we need to think about it. I'll talk to a few people. And that other thing he showed us – you know, when he was talking about globalisation, might be useful . . . possibly . . .'
Daniel: 'So how are you going to use his stuff in the values implementation, Jan?'
Jan: 'Oh . . . Well . . . I . . . Hang on a minute, he didn't really talk about culture change at all, did he?'
Jennifer: 'Come to think of it . . . No he didn't really . . .'
Jan: 'Where were those questions I asked him?' (*pauses to riffle though her notes*) 'I remember *asking* him these, but I can't really

remember what he . . . if he . . .'

Jennifer: (*looking over Jan's shoulder*) 'I don't think he really talked about any of those.'

Daniel: 'I remember the way you kept going back to your questions, trying to wrestle the conversation back to values . . . but he always seemed to change the subject back to his own thing . . .'

Jan: (*visibly grumpy*) 'Hmmph. Well, that was a bit of an intellectual's day out. We had a lovely time but I didn't really get any further in implementing these values, did I?'

Daniel: 'Oh well, the day hasn't gone to waste. At least we learned lots about other things.'

(Daniel has an enviable outlook on life).

Well, guru or not, he didn't get the job, because he *could not sell us what we needed*. So the final rule is:

Rule No. 8: Sell your clients what they need

There is a chance, however minuscule, that your client is not an idiot. It could happen that they know better than you what they need, what they want and what will work in their organisation. Find out what this is, and if you can sell it to them, go ahead. Don't try to sell them irrelevant information.

Four Golden Rules for Clients

Let's not give management consultants any more of a slating. I have been a consultant for long enough to recognise that there are lots of mistakes which clients make too. And, speaking as a client, I know there were things that I could have done differently and better. So this section gives advice to clients of consultants everywhere. Just because you're holding the purse strings it doesn't mean you can't contribute to a more harmonious consulting relationship. However, in recognition of just how important you are, there are less rules for clients than for consultants.

Culture change and organisation development offer huge potential for consultants to add value. A wide range of skill sets is required, and a vast array of consultants, mostly small or niche players, compete for work in this field: psychologists, communications consultants, 'change management' specialists, academics, HR professionals, facilitators and strategists, to name but a few. When faced with this variety of skills, not to mention the assortment of personalities which accompany them, you have to think very carefully about what you need. Do you need some creative ideas? Do you need a sounding board? (I didn't say sounding boards weren't useful . . .) Do you need a spare pair of hands? Someone to produce tangible deliverables? Someone to offer practical ideas and help? Which is it? What you need to do is live up to the final challenge we just posed to consultants: know what you want. So here is the first rule:

Rule No. 1: Know what you are looking for
Be as clear as you can about what you need. When you have a job to do, think about the nature of it and the skills needed, and explain carefully to candidates what you want.

Working with a wide range of consultants is very rewarding – you won't be bored. In my experience, the best ideas have often come from the most unexpected quarters – no doubt because you get a fresh perspective from the people who are most unlike yourself. So while you should think carefully about what it is you want, sometimes it pays to keep an open mind (and open ears) about who can help you. You need to keep up-to-date on what is available in the consulting marketplace. Which brings us to the second rule:

Rule No. 2: Know what's out there
Familiarise yourself with the consulting offerings in the market. Build relationships with a number of consultants. Find out what they do and how they do it, even if you do not have an immediate need for their services. Getting to know them now will make the selection process a lot less risky when you do need them. Keep an open mind about who can help you too – don't rule out altogether unconventional sources.

I have at times asked consultants to do the impossible. They failed. There are certain things which external consultants simply can't do.

Mind reading for example. One consultancy which helped me on the toolkit witnessed how almost everything they produced got completely rewritten. This was not because they were bad consultants, but because there came a point when the work simply had to be done by someone from within KPMG who was wholly familiar with the culture, language and idiosyncrasies of the firm. What is this telling us?

Rule No. 3: Recognise that there are some things you need to do yourself
Some tasks require inside knowledge of your organisation and like it or not, consultants will not be able to help you. Sometimes there are advantages in using an external consultant over an internal resource, but remember that the opposite is also true.

Consultants will need time to learn about your organisation. They will not be highly effective from Day One. To help you, they need to know about your business, its history, the people, the culture, structure, procedures, systems, processes and so on. You can help them learn about this by taking time to brief them properly, by getting people to speak to them, by giving them background information and by patiently answering what might seem to you like stupid questions. This is very time-consuming initially, but it will make for a much happier and more productive consulting relationship in the long run. The final rule is therefore:

Rule No. 4: Help your consultants
Help build a mutually beneficial consulting relationship. It's not as if you are setting your consultants an intelligence test. Brief them properly. Explain things. Give them every opportunity to succeed. Be co-operative. Give them feedback. And give them time.

A final word
In this chapter, we have looked at where KPMG has got to in its culture change effort as well as some of the lessons learned along the way. While KPMG has made huge progress, we admit freely that there has not yet been a miraculous transformation of our culture.

And, not surprisingly, the process has not been without frustrations and setbacks. Such difficulties are normal. Anyone who has ever managed a big change programme will recall more than one occasion when they felt like throwing in the towel or hitting someone. Being a change agent calls for a fair amount of resilience. So how do you survive this role with your sanity intact and without incurring any charges of grievous bodily harm?

First: be positive. Some setbacks along the way are inevitable. That's just life. But there is a way around every setback, or there are other things you could be doing in the meantime. Sometimes something which looks like a problem often has a positive side. Looking at things in a positive way will help you to persist.

Secondly: if you truly believe in what you are doing, you will surface again quickly from any blows you sustain along the way.

Thirdly: be realistic about expectations. It is a fact that most change agents are idealists at heart, passionate crusaders for improving life in organisations. This is in general a good thing, but at the same time you have to be careful not to fall victim to disillusionment. Be aware that culture change does not happen overnight and that there is a great deal of work involved in the process. Don't be put off, but be prepared.

In other words: be realistic, but optimistic too.

Chapter 6

CULTURE CHANGE FOR EVERYONE

What puts culture on the agenda of so many different organisations? And once it is there, what general principles can be applied to achieve any desired changes? What can be learned from KPMG's process which could be applied in any organisation, whether it is in professional services or not – whether it is in business or not? What about small companies, start-ups, non-profit and public sector organisations, to name but a few?

While it is true that every organisation is in a unique situation, many of the overarching issues that arise in culture change are the same, irrespective of the organisation's size or type. Because of this, the lessons gained from KPMG's programme can be applied equally well in a wider context to give guidance on culture change for everyone.

In this chapter, we examine the predicaments of different types of organisation, drawing out common themes and looking more generally at how culture can be changed, revitalised or strengthened. We examine the wider implications of culture change and its significance in shaping the organisations of the future.

New challenges, old problems?
Never has the world of work teemed with so many different opportunities and choices. The very nature of organisations is changing dramatically, with new types evolving all the time: mammoth corporations are born as huge companies marry, small start-ups rocket to success in minimal time, networks spring up,

alliances are formed, functions are outsourced, the virtual marketplace is populated. (And by the way, the traditional bricks-and-mortar organisation continues to exist alongside all this.)

Many people wonder what can be taken with us into this world – what do we know about leadership, management and motivation that still holds true? The nature of organisations might be changing dramatically, but human nature is not. Leaders in organisations still need to create alignment, inspire people, maintain focus and improve performance just as before. The challenges are the same as ever, but the changing patterns in the work environment add to their complexity.

Let's look at some of the issues facing different types of organisation, and the role culture has to play:

Large, mature organisations
Most large organisations whose cultures have become well-established over time will be able to identify with the issues that KPMG faced as it set off on the path to culture change. A mature culture can be hard to change simply because it has persisted for so long. But often, there is no choice. Cultural problems, if they remain unresolved, can eventually choke a mature organisation. Some of the more common issues are as follows:

- Large companies often have diverse businesses or divisions to contend with as well as numerous geographic locations. There will be a range of operations, each of which will have its own sub-culture. Sub-cultures need to be allowed to flourish in so far as they support real and necessary differences in – working patterns and markets: for example, you would want your accountants to be more conservative and risk-averse than, say, your marketing department. But interfaces between sub-cultures need to be carefully managed: if different departments lose sight of the organisation's overall values, differences in sub-culture can become exaggerated, and lead to friction, in-fighting and fragmentation. Leaders need to be sensitive to how the culture is developing in various parts of the business, and always ensure that there is a bigger picture of the culture which unites everyone across all of the organisation.

- Globalisation is often a major concern of large organisations. Many companies are already represented in different countries, and are struggling to make sure they look, feel and act global while still gaining acceptance in local markets. Again this calls for clarity about which beliefs and practices are common across the globe, what is set in stone and what can be tailored to suit local needs. Leaders need to maintain alignment with the basic guiding principles dictated by the organisation's vision and values while at the same time demonstrating an understanding of how these will be manifested in different national cultures.

- Mature organisations can often have ingrained patterns of behaviour that no longer fit with the expectations and demands of their customers and potential employees. They may then find themselves losing more and more key accounts or struggling to attract good people and retain their best staff. Many are seeking to modernise in order to overcome these problems and assure their competitive position. Such organisations often find that over time they have lost sight of their purpose and values and allowed themselves to drift. They might not necessarily need to change in a radical way, but rather to re-articulate what is important to them, to strengthen and revitalise their cultures.

There is a commonly held belief that only young organisations can mould their cultures and that the culture of a more mature organisation is impossible to alter. It is true that a well-established culture is slower to change and that many mature organisations find themselves struggling to shake off the legacy of past behaviours, but there are also distinct advantages to having a mature culture. In a long-established organisation, employees share a sense of history. There is more common ground, this brings people together and in some ways enables them to recognise more quickly what their purpose and values should be.

Mergers and acquisitions

We see a great deal of consolidation in the business environment today. Organisations which are already bigger than anything we could have imagined ten years ago are combining to form even bigger corporations, while companies in growing markets are vacuuming innovative start-ups at an amazing rate. Around one in three employees will at some point in their careers find themselves in the midst of a merger situation. News of mergers and takeover bids is reported almost every day in the financial pages of the newspaper. You would think that with all this merging and acquisition going on, someone would have figured out how to get it right. Yet an estimated 50% of all mergers and acquisitions fail to meet their objectives. Why is this? Opinion differs on exact figures, but the research shows that the causes of failure are generally not due to poor strategic fit or badly executed deal negotiation. The cause of failure is often – some say mainly – culture. In other words, when the papers have all been signed, the two new marriage partners find that they just hate living together, and the grief that this causes can quickly negate the benefits which the deal set out to achieve.

Although 'culture clash' is known to be a major cause of failure in mergers and acquisitions, it is rarely handled adequately as a risk factor in acquisitions strategies. Perhaps this is because people find culture hard to understand, and have difficulties in determining the criteria by which they should assess their acquisition target's or their merger partner's culture. Assessing the culture of another organisation is certainly no mean task, but given the failure statistics, it seems that it is just as important as carrying out a thorough due diligence (and no one would think of proceeding in negotiations without the latter). New ways need to be found to assess cultural fit, and some of the approaches presented in this book would not be a bad starting point.

The irony is that while most acquirers might be happy to look at ways to assess their target's culture, they often do not understand sufficiently *their own* culture and the impact that it will have on the success of the deal. Any organisation that wishes to merge with or acquire another needs to recognise that culture change is inevitable no matter what the nature of the deal. And like any other organisation facing cultural change, the starting point needs to be clear. In other words, whether the relationship is that of acquirer and target, or a marriage of equals, an in-depth understanding of the existing culture in *both* organisations is needed.

Mergers and acquisitions are hotbeds for cultivating 'them and us' attitudes. It is natural that when people feel at risk they cling on to old values and beliefs, and even years after a merger, it is not uncommon to find that there are still distinct, rival cultures operating within the newly formed organisation. Cultural differences are often misinterpreted, and when people are feeling suspicious and insecure anyway (a justifiable reaction in many merger situations), misunderstandings can quickly escalate into more serious problems. Friction between competing cultures can turn destructive and have a negative impact both on the work environment and on overall business performance.

Therefore choices need to be made early on about how culture will be handled post-merger. If one culture is likely to predominate in the merged organisation, then plans need to be made for how people from the disappearing culture will be integrated or, to use a psychological term, 'socialised'. A better idea might be to involve people from both of the original organisations in using some of the approaches we have discussed in this book to build a new, truly shared culture in the merged organisation.

Whatever approach is taken in the end, one thing is for sure: culture clashes in merger situations are to be ignored at the management's peril.

Non-profit organisations
When I was a student at business school there were often heated debates (mostly initiated by the students from public sector organisations) about whether the commercial principles which were being taught would apply just as well to non-profit organisations. There is no doubt in my mind that there are some variations in how organisations in the private and public sector can be run, but when it comes to cultural issues, I believe there are more similarities than differences.

Management and leadership issues in non-profit organisations are the same as in business. Leaders have to provide direction just as much as they do in a commercial company, and a clear sense of purpose and a shared set of values can be developed in exactly the same way for a public sector body as for a business.

As in business, large non-profit organisations are very diverse and there may be powerful sub-cultures in operation. Sometimes these sub-cultures go back further than the organisation itself, and this can make it hard to maintain alignment. For example, the sub-cultures which exist in a hospital would include those associated with professions – medicine and nursing – as well as those which grow up naturally around wards and other departments. It is important that anyone running such an organisation understands the complexities of sub-cultures and ensures that people still focus ultimately on the overall goals and aspirations of the organisation. How different is that from business? Not very. The same culture change methods apply.

Non-profit and public sector organisations also find themselves increasingly under the same pressure that businesses face: to improve efficiency and reduce costs. They may not be in direct competition with other organisations of their kind, but, particularly in Western countries, public policy changes are forcing them to act as if they were. As government subsidies decline and performance measures and scoring systems are introduced, the competition for public funding is often just as ferocious as the competition for customers in business. Public sector and non-profit organisations, like businesses, need to be fit to survive in the environment in which they operate, and this too requires the right culture.

E-business
The Internet is an organisation with its own, unique culture. An Internet consultant I know says it is like a different country, and not always a welcoming one to those who do not know its customs. It is a self-governing community with its own way of doing things, its own, weird language, and its own set of values. It is a country in which we will all have to live at least some of the time if we do not want to be left behind. Whether we are working in conventional

businesses, or whether we are involved with Internet companies, we will all have to understand and adapt to the Net just as an Englishman going to China needs to know about local customs, business etiquette and language. More so, perhaps, because while a Chinese business person may be willing to adapt and make exceptions for an English visitor, the Internet will not adapt to suit us. It is we who have to learn to fit in.

Traditional bricks-and-mortar companies have finally woken up to the fact that the Internet is not going away. They know that a time will come when they will do much of their business through this medium. Hence the rush to recruit people who are already members of this community. The implications for traditional organisations are huge: they will have to rethink the way they work and their relationships with customers, employees, suppliers and competitors. But most importantly, they will have to truly understand the culture of the Net: how to be accepted, how to make links, how to form alliances, how to trade, how to behave. Competence in the Internet world means more than just technical skills. The need for cultural awareness far exceeds any implications for technology, business processes and work policies. Successful organisations will be those who manage to become socialised in the culture of this different country.

Alongside traditional companies developing a presence on the Internet, many new organisations are being born there. These are altogether different animals from traditional bricks-and-mortar organisations. But not all are successful, and in the scramble to invest, care needs to be exercised. Few people really know how to evaluate an Internet start-up and typical models used by venture capitalists no longer apply. You might invest in something which turns out to be another Amazon.com, but then again it might be a complete flop. How can you tell the difference in the early stages? One thing which will give some clues is the culture. There is a perception that Internet companies are all out to make a quick buck and that this is the only motivation which drives them. In fact, for successful Internet companies the reverse is true. To quote Tom Jermoluk of @Home Inc, employees of e-businesses want '. . . to understand what it is they are part of and how it makes a difference'. Only a clearly defined sense of purpose and a set of deeply held shared values can provide this inspiration and motivation.

E-businesses are by their very nature less hierarchical than traditional organisations, more fluid, often more unconventional and definitely less responsive to old-fashioned approaches to management. They need to be led rather than managed, and to achieve this, a shared system of values provides the guidance which rigid rules cannot.

Every organisation needs to be able to move fast, but Internet companies probably need to be even more agile than that. We have at various times in this book discussed how a strong culture enables an organisation to change more swiftly and surely. A clear, shared set of values provides people with a sound basis for making faster and better decisions. A strong culture is not a 'nice to have' in e-business, it is perhaps not even a source of competitive advantage: it is an essential for survival.

New organisations
Any new organisation, whether it is an e-business or not, has a tremendous opportunity to build a positive culture from the very start. Just as Hewlett and Packard decided what values would guide their company from its humble beginnings in a garage to becoming a successful international corporation, so the leaders of start-ups can consciously mould the culture of their growing organisations.

Everyone starting a business should think carefully about the purpose of that business and the values which they will live by. They should apply the tests which we applied in KPMG when thinking about core purpose – what would the world be missing if this company did not exist? And they should also think about core values – the enduring guiding principles which the organisation will never give up – as well as identifying the behaviours which support them. They should then constantly reinforce their values in their actions, policies and decisions.

Government offices and political parties
If ever a decision was values-based, it is the decision made by a voter in a democratic electoral system. Voters rarely examine in detail the

election manifestos of different political parties and make calculated choices: instead, they tend to vote for the political party whose values appear to resonate most with their own, personal values. The problem is that these days, as more and more political parties seem to jostle for position at the centre right, as accusations of sleaze become so commonplace that we are bored by them, and as 'spin-doctor' becomes a recognised profession, it can be quite hard for the average voter to identify politicians' true values. We could all do with more clarity and definition of the different parties' beliefs. Otherwise there is a risk, as we see happening in parts of the world, that power is suddenly grabbed by extremist groups who aren't afraid to take a stand.

Many political organisations suffer from a lack of alignment. We see this in their sometimes contradictory actions, policy U-turns and failure to achieve continuity. Clarity of vision is needed more than ever. Values help create alignment but still allow a system that degree of diversity which is essential in a democratic system. They are the basic assumptions around which all other debate can range freely and where, in spite of healthy differences, a common purpose can be achieved. As in any other organisation, clarity about which values and beliefs are shared and non-negotiable, and which are not, might be helpful to political parties.

Do party policies and new legislation really change the way we do things? I recently heard an interesting debate about passing a new law. The proposed law aimed to legislate against the with-holding of certain information in government offices. Someone was arguing that it was not the law, but the *culture* of the government office in question which needed to change. He pointed out that if the law were to be passed, it might make potential offenders even *more* cautious about divulging too much, thus worsening the situation. This argument could of course be taken to a silly extreme, which is to say that there is no point in passing *any* legislation and it is all a question of culture. Of course society needs laws. But there is a very valid point here nevertheless: changing a law constitutes no more than changing an artefact of national culture. Changing legislation enables people who break a particular law to be charged after the event. In this way, undesirable behaviours in society can be reduced. But isn't there more to it than that? What about looking at what else could be changed in order to eradicate undesirable behaviours? What cultural changes could be made to ensure that the law need not be enforced in the first place? In attempting to bring about lasting positive changes to society, we could all perhaps benefit from understanding in more depth the cultural systems in operation.

Different organisations, same solutions?
Although we have looked at organisations with different forms, there is a commonality in the issues which they face. These issues may take on different guises or have different causes, but most organisations, irrespective of their size or type, will recognise at least some of the following and find solutions to them in culture change.

Defining what you are
Whether an organisation is just starting up, or whether it has drifted for so long that it has begun to lose sight of why it exists and how it goes about its work, its people need to know, at the deepest level, what it is there for and what it stands for. Only a lasting set of values, together with a clear statement of purpose, can provide these. And both have to be genuinely embedded in the culture of the organisation: it is not enough just to say the words.

In a mature organisation, how do you know how clear your purpose and values are? Ask a few people to articulate them for you. Not just leaders: everyone should know and understand what the company is all about. So whether you are in a Board meeting, or talking to the guy in the post room, if no consistent answers are being found to these questions, or if people are repeating slogans at you which they clearly don't believe, then it is time to think about doing something like KPMG did.

Organisations which are starting out have the luxury of creating the culture they want. They can paint a rich picture of their desired culture just as we described in the early chapters of this book, and then put in place the mechanisms to ensure that the culture is put into practice. This sounds ideal, but start-ups beware: you might not be starting with a clean sheet of paper. Remnants of the cultures you have left behind in previous occupations might come back to haunt you. How often have we all seen colleagues, sick of life in large organisations, break away to found small businesses only to recreate on a lesser scale many of the things which irritated them in the first place? Culture is sneaky. It is a habit which is hard to shake off. Even those who have an apparent 'blank slate' need to invest time in thinking through not just the culture they want, but also how the culture they have come from might affect them. They need to be aware of what behaviours might, in spite of the best intentions, trip them up. And they constantly, consistently and passionately need to reinforce the tenets of the desired culture.

Managing culture across boundaries
Whether coping with the aftermath of a merger, grappling with issues of geography, or simply dealing with inevitable clashes between departments or units, leaders of organisations at all levels need to understand how to manage differences in culture. A deep understanding of culture is needed. Many of the methods in this book can be used on a smaller scale, for example to examine how sub-cultures differ between units. The important thing is that differences are identified and discussed – a first step in resolving difficulties.

Alignment v. empowerment
There is a dilemma about creating alignment in an organisation while also allowing empowerment to flourish. How can you ensure that people all act in an acceptable way while they also have free rein to do their own thing?

Maintaining a balance between alignment and empowerment is perceived as difficult. Alignment is often mistaken for the imposition of controls. These are not the same. There is a difference between dictating to people what to do and trusting them to do the right thing. But how can you be sure that you can trust them to do the right thing? How will they know what that is?

It is possible to create an organisation which is aligned and yet empowered. The key is to manage culture at the correct level. A set of core values – strictly adhered to, unchanging and, once articulated, non-negotiable – is an essential ingredient for creating alignment. Contrary to what you might think, these are also essential ingredients for empowerment, but in addition to being strict, unchanging and non-negotiable, the core values have to be truly understood, shared and believed in passionately by all the people in the organisation. Values are 'the pin that holds the pendulum'. Values provide a discipline – basic tenets which, once they are understood, empower people to make better and bigger decisions. So to create alignment in an organisation, the solution is not to impose a rigid set of rules or introduce hundreds of standards, that would kill empowerment for sure (and a few other things besides, such as motivation and morale). The answer is instead to look at creating a set of shared values, and, rather than enforcing them by law, to make sure that these are fully understood and written in the hearts and minds of employees.

Strong cultures v. diversity
Most organisations recognise that in our global, ever-changing world, diversity is an essential ingredient for a successful business. An organisation is so much richer, and so much better at matching its target markets, if it employs people of different races, genders, ages, professions, skills and personalities. But most organisations recognise that a strong culture is also essential to improving business performance. Strong cultures can be cult-like, can't they? Where does that leave room for diversity?

I once had a bizarre conversation with someone at KPMG about their worry that if we promoted our desired culture too strongly, our people would all think and behave in the same way. Because of this, they felt we would lose the healthy differences in perspective which we need to provide creative or innovative solutions to problems. Once I had got over hooting with laughter at the idea that KPMG might ever get to the stage where everyone thought and behaved the same, I gave the question some more serious consideration. I concluded that there is a big difference between believing in the same thing and *being* the same. In a strong culture, there is still room for diversity to flourish. The behaviours dictated by the company's values are those which people should have in common, and likewise, there should be a set of behaviours which are universally unacceptable. But these two are just tiny subsets of the entire range of human behaviour. There is still plenty of room for individualism and diversity. Again it is a question of the level at which you manage culture: diverse individuals can still share a small number of core beliefs about what is right and wrong. In fact, if they do share a set of core values, they learn to trust one another and this leads to *more* tolerance of differences. As with empowerment, diversity does not flourish in organisations which impose lists of strict rules. But it flourishes absolutely in organisations which have a deeply held set of shared values.

Everything you always wanted to know about culture change

A great deal of this book has focused on the *process* of culture change: the basic three-phase approach of truly understanding the existing culture, defining the desired culture, and then carrying out the organisational and behavioural changes to make the desired culture real. This is a basic, reproducible process which can be used in any organisation.

Of course there is more to it than chugging through a basic reproducible process. There are a few further principles which anyone undertaking culture change should know.

Answer the big questions

There are three basic questions you need to bear in mind when conducting culture change:

- Why?
- What?
- How?

Tempted as I am to leave it at that, I'll elaborate a little:

Why?
It's that question again – 'why bother?' Why would you want to put your organisation through the throes of culture change when there

are altogether more pleasant ways of spending time and money? The answer to the 'why' question is the business case: the rock-solid reason for conducting culture change. If you really need culture change in your organisation it should be glaringly obvious to you because of what is going on around you. You should be able to gather sound evidence and convincing data to build a compelling case for change. Think about the following questions:

- What is unnerving the organisation's leaders? What threats are out there in the business environment which a culture change will deflect?
- What opportunities will you miss by not changing? What is so tempting, so attractive, to capture, that people would be prepared to undertake culture change for it, including the difficult and often painful process of changing themselves?
- What will be the consequences of *not* changing? Will the organisation fall over? Or is it more a case of passing on a 'nice to have'? If you had to score the consequences of staying as you are on a scale of 1 to 5, where 5 is 'complete disaster' and 1 is 'minor irritation', how would you rate?

Even when you have answered these questions, it is not enough. As well as sound evidence, the business case needs to communicate a real sense of urgency. So look at the answers to the above questions and ask yourself, 'How soon must all this be resolved?' Are you talking about distant threats and opportunities, or are you talking about things that need to start happening now? Inevitably, people will find it hard to get worried about a 'complete disaster' predicted to happen in ten years' time, but they might be motivated to do something if a smaller disaster, or a golden opportunity, were just around the corner. Of course, because culture change is a slow process, you have to start early. This means that you will have to build your case with care, remembering to balance implications and timings in constructing your arguments.

What?
So what was it you were about to change? You need clarity about

what needs to happen, and this requires you to have a precise picture of both the existing and desired cultures. Then the things that will enable you to migrate from one to the other will become apparent.

Make sure that your understanding of the existing culture is deep enough, and that your picture of the desired culture is richly painted. In other words, include not only values statements, but also specific descriptions of behaviour in both. And when it comes to describing the desired culture, remember to outline the outcomes and benefits you will expect by including statements about 'how we will know when we have got there'. Help people to visualise what it will be like: not only for the sake of clarity, but also to inspire and motivate them to support the change.

Look at the descriptions of the existing and desired cultures and if you do not recognise anything from the former in the latter, be worried. Don't allow people to throw away what is good about the existing culture, and don't imagine that it is possible to transform a culture completely. Be realistic and think about how the desired culture can evolve from the existing culture: what needs to be learned, what needs to be unlearned, what needs to be broadened or reinterpreted, what needs to stay the same. Culture is a living thing. You cannot kill it and hope to bring it back to life in another guise. Like a living thing you need to understand it, mould it, help it to learn new ways. Culture change is a gradual process and requires sensitivity as well as a sound measure of good sense.

There might be many answers to the 'what' question: too many things that could be changed. Pick the ones which will best address the business case, the ones that will make the most difference. After that, pick the ones which might not have so much impact but are easy to do. Don't bother with the ones which have minor impact and are difficult to do: culture change presents you with more than enough challenges to keep you occupied.

How?

How do you go about culture change? There are a number of principles which should operate throughout the process. These are the ones without which we would have failed at KPMG, and I cannot imagine a culture change programme where they would not apply.

- Sponsorship needs to be strong, particularly from the top. It is vital that the leadership team champions the values in their words *and* actions. Culture change is particularly difficult for sponsors, because as champions of the change they also have to be exemplary role models. Your friends on the leadership team are probably no more gifted at personal transformation than the rest of us, so they will need a lot of support in this. You might at times need to challenge, coach and remind leaders of what it means to be an effective sponsor. This can be a tough call, and you need to ensure that your relationship with them permits you to do it.
- Involve people from the day-to-day business as much as possible. Remember that it is *their* beliefs and aspirations that you are trying to influence. The success of the programme is dependent on their buy-in. You will have to get as many people as possible to work on the culture throughout the three stages of the process, and you should aim to get a fair representation of views. You will fail to define or implement a culture which means anything to the majority of people in the organisation if you set up a small, elite team to work in isolation. The business world has many, many examples of senior managers who have unused values statements tucked away in their drawers. Don't be like one of them.
- Integrate your programme as fully as possible with the ongoing activities of the organisation. In other words, your aim should be to make the new values so embedded in the work of the leadership and support functions that your 'culture change' programme becomes invisible to the average employee. In the initial stages, you will inevitably need to run distinct 'culture change' initiatives to determine your position and tackle immediate issues. But as time progresses, the more you can do within existing structures and initiatives, and the less you need to set up separate 'values'

projects, the better. The goal of any change agent should be to work themselves out of a job.

- See the whole picture. Make links between culture, strategy and operations. Build understanding of how the drive to a new culture influences strategic decisions. On an operational level, ensure that the behaviours which support the new culture are supported by the organisation's business processes. Ensure that the culture change agenda and the business agenda are one. In KPMG, we did this by using existing events – Board meetings, development programmes and conferences – to work on our culture. In this way, the culture change effort became integral to strategy development and implementation. In your own organisation, look at what means are available to you to make sure that culture is correctly positioned. Don't fall into the common trap of culture change being perceived as something separate from real life, an afterthought or a management whim. Make it clear that culture change is gritty and real and a fundamental part of the business agenda.

- Remember that your culture is unique to your organisation. It is a precious thing which is all yours. It is core to the organisation's very being. So don't be tempted to 'borrow' values from other successful companies, no matter how good they sound. It is so important that your organisation's values are authentic and truly believed by your company's employees. If your people believed passionately in another organisation's values, then that should be their next career move! And because your company values are all your own, don't ask an external person to formulate them for you. Ask external consultants to help you facilitate the process if you need them, but work on the *content* yourselves.

- Communication is key – plan your communication effort and then multiply it by a factor of ten. If you think this is exaggerating, answer honestly these questions: how many of the corporate communications which *you* receive go straight into the wastepaper bin? How often does your mind wander when your CEO is giving his or her annual pep-talk? Have you ever got around to watching that communications video which your company sent out to your home, or did you try to tape last night's episode of *ER* over it? The need for communication is *always* underestimated. At KPMG we too could have done much better. Communicate lots – more than lots – and think of what less conventional and more readily accessible approaches you might use to engage your target audiences.

- Think about how you will continue to stimulate interest throughout the process. Culture change is a long haul and your organisation's employees are only human – they get bored. Boredom causes us to forget and forgetting will kill your programme. How do you maintain interest? One way is to include creative or unconventional methods in your approach. Innovate. Surprise people. Look outside your organisation to more unconventional sources of ideas. At KPMG we drew some of our inspiration from the arts: drama and design. And we pushed the boundaries back in the way we facilitated events. We made people play games and we made people laugh. There are so many ways of keeping a long programme alive and it is essential that you consciously build these in to your approach. Another way to keep the programme alive is to manage the timing of changes you make to artefacts of the culture – especially the ones which have particular symbolic significance. Don't change all your artefacts at once. Instead, time changes to coincide with points when your programme might be flagging, especially when those changes might be perceived as dramatic. Of course the effects of changing artefacts will be short-lived, but who cares? Your aim is simply to wake people up and say, 'Yo-hoo, it's still here, don't forget the culture change!' All you are trying to do is inject some life into the programme, so make sure you exploit every one of these opportunities and continually reinforce the message.
- Don't wimp out. Or rather, don't let your sponsors wimp

out on dealing with obstacles to the desired culture. You can probably think of at least ten things which could be done straight away to eliminate obstructions to your desired culture. You just need to make sure that people in your organisation, especially the leaders, have the guts to follow through. Structures or rules which undermine the new culture need to be changed or removed – sometimes even certain people, if they cannot change their behaviours, need to go as well. Likewise, everything which supports, and everyone who embodies the new culture, should be upheld and promoted as positive examples. It is important to the success of the programme that these issues are dealt with properly. Everyone will be watching and waiting to see whether it is 'safe' to practise the new culture, whether they will benefit from behaving in the new way. They will also be curious about whether it is still OK to carry on in the old ways – as it is always more comfortable not to change. In building credibility for the new ways, one relapse can undo all the good achieved by ten positive actions. It is time to get tough and show a clear commitment to the new culture.

- Have a process, but remember that you are not married to it. If things start to go wrong, or if a better opportunity presents itself, you can change it. There is no neat, sequential approach which will guarantee success. In real life you will be subjected to all sorts of constraints, influences and opportunities. Your process might sometimes look a mess, but that's OK. As long as you have your goals clearly in mind, and if you remain sensitive to the peculiarities, moods and situations in your organisation, you will be able to develop an approach which is flexible but also rigorous enough to succeed.

- No matter how fast-moving your organisation may perceive itself to be, culture change will be slow. Manage expectations: you will experience no dramatic changes overnight. Be realistic about what you can do and remember that even small changes in culture can make a big difference to the business.

- Be clear and be practical. Culture change is often regarded as nebulous, 'touchy feely' and mysterious. It is your job to dispel that myth. You have frameworks now to talk about culture in an informed, no-nonsense way. And you have ideas for a host of actions which even the most traditional managers would recognise as practical. You have the tools and techniques to prove the sceptics wrong. Culture change is about doing – not about hypothesising.

Culture change for everyone

In this book I have done my best to explain what you can do to create lasting culture change in a real-life organisation – not one which has already built a superstar culture, nor one which was in dire straits and in desperate need of a turnaround. I have written it in this way because I believe that the majority of organisations fall somewhere in between these two extremes. They are neither shining examples worthy of tracts in textbooks, nor are they a dying breed whose entrails give us clues about what *not* to do. Most organisations have a culture which enables them to survive, and perhaps even do well. Their cultures feature many characteristics which are not so bad. Inevitably, much of what constitutes their cultures will be extremely valuable and worth preserving. But there will also be a few things about their cultures which are not so good, and which get in the way of better business performance. There will undoubtedly be elements of their cultures which they have good reason for wanting to change, and this book will, I hope, help them to make such changes.

As well as containing the odd foray into the field of organisational science, this book drew on our day-to-day experiences at KPMG to see what can be done to revitalise the culture of other, real-life organisations. In telling KPMG's story, many concepts, tips, tools and techniques came to light. Not all of these will be relevant to every organisation, and different readers will have learned different things from this book. That's fine, because, at the risk of repeating myself yet again, this text was never intended to be a standard book for culture change.

However, there are three fundamental messages which I do hope every reader will take away, and will use as they address issues of culture change in their diverse organisations around the world.

These are simple messages – no in-depth insights or ground-breaking concepts here – but paying attention to them will enable anyone to see through the complexities of a real-life culture change programme. Here they are:

First, before you embark on a process of culture change, make sure you understand what organisational culture *is*. Before you try to describe the culture of your own organisation, or attempt to define how it should look, make sure that you and those around you have an in-depth insight into culture in general: how it is structured, where it comes from, how it can be changed. Check that you are all using the same words and understanding the same things when you talk about values, behaviours and artefacts. Ensure that people understand how deep culture goes, what is conscious, what is unconscious, what can be altered and what is enduring. So many culture change initiatives fail or are misguided because of a lack of common understanding about all these things, even though it is not difficult to get them right. Become an authority on organisational culture, and share this knowledge with the people around you.

Secondly, understand your own organisation: not only its culture, but its dynamics, its history, what will work and what will not work. Your organisation is unique and you will need to develop a unique approach if you wish to effect anything more than the most superficial of culture changes. This sounds complicated, but you are lucky, because all you need to know is already contained within your own organisation. The people in your organisation have all the knowledge and capability needed to develop and implement the right culture. There might be no guaranteed recipe for culture change, but if you look carefully, you will have all the ingredients you need to succeed.

Thirdly, culture change is not rocket science. Nor is it something which belongs only in the domain of managerial wizards. It's much more simple than that. When I started out on KPMG's path to culture change, I sought the advice of many people: business leaders, consultants, academics and management gurus. I was looking for the Holy Grail of culture change, the ultimate insight into How to Make It Happen. In spite of searching far and wide I found that no one, no matter how revered and intelligent, could enlighten me. I began to suspect the worst: i.e. that nobody really knows the single best route to culture change. So I just started to do some of the things described in earlier chapters of this book, and after a while, I realised that there is no great insight, no magic formula for culture change.

In fact, it is not true that nobody really knows how to bring about culture change. *Everyone* knows how to bring about culture change. They might not know they know it, but they know it all the same. The secret is just to *do stuff that helps*. Culture change is an exercise in practicality. There is no mystique – it just requires a lot of common sense. Optimism, persistence and determination help, but other than that, anyone who understands these three simple messages can lead a culture change.

Is this going to make life in organisations any easier? Maybe. Maybe not. How often do we hear people say things like:

'The only real solution to the problems in that company/ school/police force/public service is culture change!'

This is a difficult argument to refute, but since many people at present have no idea about how to bring about culture change, it rarely results in progress. It may even be a good excuse to do nothing. If, however, we acknowledge that there is no mystery involved in changing an organisation's culture, we have to face up to the fact that we *can* tackle problems which in the past we may have avoided. In other words, we now have no excuse for tolerating dead-end, stifling, unhappy organisations. Whether culture change is undertaken on a large scale, as it was at KPMG, or whether the scope is much smaller, we all have the ability to make a significant difference. With a firm grasp of the nature of culture, an awareness of the basics of organisation dynamics, and a few ideas, tools and techniques, anyone can take on the challenge of culture change. Unless we choose to live as hermits, we all live with organisations, and indeed many of us spend a large part of our lives inside them. We owe it to ourselves to revitalise our organisations, to give them new energy and effectiveness and to re-awaken their living culture.

INDEX